CREATIVE
HOMEOWNER®

ULTIMATE
WATERFRONT
HOME PLANS

Book content provided by Design America, Inc., St. Louis, MO.

Current Printing (last digit)
10 9 8 7 6 5 4 3 2 1

Printed in China

Ultimate Waterfront Home Plans
ISBN-13: 978-1-58011-871-2

CREATIVE HOMEOWNER®
www.creativehomeowner.com

Creative Homeowner books are distributed by

Fox Chapel Publishing
903 Square Street
Mount Joy, PA 17552
www.FoxChapelPublishing.com

The homes featured on the cover are: top, Plan #F12-080D-0012 on page 53; right, top to bottom: Plan #F12-058D-0202 on page 29; Plan #F12-091D-0506 on page 40; Plan #F12-058D-0243 on page 96. Unless noted, all images copyrighted by the designer/architect.

The home featured on page 1 is Plan #F12-056D-0120 on page 21.

CONTENTS

Top to bottom: Plan #F12-024D-0008 on page 45; Plan #F12-101D-0155 on page 32; Plan #F12-128D-0060 on page 17; Plan #F12-141D-0025 on page 107; Plan #F12-024D-0813 on page 26; Plan #F12-056D-0098 on page 52.

getting started:

what's the right **PLAN** for you?

Choosing a house design is exciting, but can be a difficult task. Many factors play a role in what home plan is best for you and your family. To help you get started, we have pinpointed some of the major factors to consider when searching for your dream home. Take the time to evaluate your family's needs and you will have an easier time sorting through all of the house designs offered in this book.

Budget is the first thing to consider. Many items take part in this budget, from ordering the blueprints to the last doorknob purchased. When you find the perfect house plan, visit houseplansandmore.com and get a cost-to-build estimate to ensure that the finished home will be within your cost range. A cost-to-build report is a detailed summary that gives you the total cost to build a specific home in the zip code where you're wanting to build. It is interactive allowing you to adjust labor and material costs, and it's created on

demand when ordered so all pricing is up-to-date. This valuable tool will help you know how much your dream home will cost before you buy plans (see page 138 for more information).

Family Lifestyle After your budget is deciphered, you need to assess you and your family's lifestyle needs. Think about the stage of life you are in now, and what stages you will be going through in the future. Ask yourself questions to figure out how much room you need now and if you will need room for expansion. Are you married? Do you have children? How many children do you plan on having? Are you an empty-nester? How long do you plan to live in this home?

Incorporate into your planning any frequent guests you may have, including elderly parents, grandchildren or adult children who may live with you.

Does your family entertain a lot? If so, think about the rooms you will need to do so. Will you need both formal and informal spaces? Do you need a gourmet kitchen? Do you need a game room and/ or a wet bar?

Floor Plan Layouts When looking through these home plans, imagine yourself walking through the house. Consider the flow from the entry to the living, sleeping and gathering areas. Does the layout ensure privacy for the master bedroom? Does the garage enter near the kitchen for easy unloading? Does the placement of the windows provide enough privacy from any neighboring

properties? Do you plan on using furniture you already have? Will this furniture fit in the appropriate rooms? When you find a plan you want to purchase, be sure to picture yourself actually living in it.

Exterior Spaces With many different home styles throughout ranging from Traditional to Contemporary, flip through these pages and find which Waterfront home design appeals to you the most and think about the neighborhood in which you plan to build. Also, think about how the house will fit on your site. Picture the landscaping you want to add to the lot. Using your imagination is key when choosing a home plan.

Choosing a house design can be an intimidating experience. Asking yourself these questions before you get started on the search will help you through the process. With our large selection of sizes and styles, we are certain you will find your dream home in this book.

Make A List!

Experts in the field suggest that the best way to determine your needs is to begin by listing everything you like or dislike about your current home.

10 steps to BUILDING your dream home

1 talk to a lender

If you plan to obtain a loan in order to build your new home, then it's best to find out first how much you can get approved for before selecting a home design. Knowing the financial information before you start looking for land or a home will keep you from selecting something out of your budget and turning a great experience into a major disappointment. Financing the home you plan to build is somewhat different than financing the purchase of an existing house. You're going to need thousands of dollars for land, labor, and materials. Chances are, you're going to have to borrow most of it. Therefore, you will probably need to obtain a construction loan. This is a short-term loan to pay for building your house. When the house is completed, the loan is paid off in full, usually out of the proceeds from your long-term mortgage loan.

2 determine needs

Selecting the right home plan for your needs and lifestyle requires a lot of thought. Your new home is an investment, so you should consider not only your current needs, but also your future requirements. Versatility and the potential for converting certain areas to other uses could be an important factor later on. So, an extra room for a guest or in-law may seem unnecessary now, in years to come, the idea may seem ideal. Home plans that include flex spaces or bonus rooms can also really adapt to your needs in the future.

3 choose a home site

The site for your new home will have a definite impact on the design you select. It's a good idea to select a home that will complement your site. This will save you time and money when building. Or, you can then modify a design to specifically accommodate your site. However, it will most likely make your home construction more costly than selecting a home plan suited for your lot right from the start. For example, if your land slopes, a walk-out basement works perfectly. If it's wooded, or has a lake in the back, an atrium ranch home is a perfect style to take advantage of surrounding backyard views.

SOME IMPORTANT CRITERIA TO CONSIDER WHEN SELECTING A SITE:

- Improvements will need to be made including utilities, sidewalks and driveways
- Convenience of the lot to work, school, shops, etc.
- Zoning requirements and property tax amounts
- Soil conditions at your future site
- Make sure the person or firm that sells you the land owns it free and clear

4 select a home design

We've chosen the "best of the best" of the Waterfront home plans found at houseplansandmore.com to be featured in this book. With over 20,000 home plans from the best architects and designers across the country, this book includes the best variety of styles and sizes to suit the needs and tastes of a broad spectrum of homeowners.

5 get the cost to build

If you feel you have found "the" home, then before taking the step of purchasing house plans, order an estimated cost-to-build report for the exact zip code where you plan to build. Requesting this custom cost report created specifically for you will help educate you on all costs associated with building your new home. Simply order this report and gain knowledge of the material and labor cost associated with the home you love. Not only does the report allow you to choose the quality of the materials, you can also select options in every aspect of the project from lot condition to contractor fees. This report will allow you to successfully manage your construction budget in all areas, clearly see where the majority of the costs lie, and save you money from start to finish.

A COST-TO-BUILD REPORT WILL DETERMINE THE OVERALL COST OF YOUR NEW HOME INCLUDING THESE 5 MAJOR EXPENSE CATEGORIES:

- Land
- Foundation
- Materials
- General Contractor's fee - Some rules-of-thumb that you may find useful are: (a) the total labor cost will generally run a little higher than your total material cost, but it's not unusual for a builder or general contractor to charge 15-20% of the combined cost for managing the overall project.
- Site improvements - don't forget to add in the cost of your site improvements such as utilities, driveway, sidewalks, landscaping, etc.

6 hire a contractor

If you're inexperienced in construction, you'll probably want to hire a general contractor to manage the project. If you do not know a reputable general contractor, begin your search by contacting your local Home Builders Association to get references. Many states require building contractors to be licensed. If this is the case in your state, its licensing board is another referral source. Finding a reputable, quality-minded contractor is a key factor in ensuring that your new home is well constructed and is finished on time and within budget. It can be a smart decision to discuss the plan you like with your builder prior to ordering plans. They can guide you into choosing the right type of plan package option especially if you intend on doing some customizing to the design.

7 customizing

Sometimes your general contractor may want to be the one who makes the mod-

ifications you want to the home you've selected. But, sometimes they want to receive the plans ready to build. That is why we offer home plan modification services. Please see page 141 for specific information on the customizing process and how to get a free quote on the changes you want to make to a home before you buy the plans.

8 order plans

If you've found the home and are ready to order blueprints, we recommend ordering the PDF file format, which offers the most flexibility. A PDF file format will be emailed to you when you order, and it includes a copyright release from the designer, meaning you have the legal right to make changes to the plan if necessary as well as print out as many copies of the plan as you need for building the home one-time. You will be happy to

have your blueprints saved electronically so they can easily be shared with your contractor, subcontractors, lender and local building officials. We do, however, offer several different types of plan package depending on your needs, so please refer to page 139 for all plan options available and choose the best one for your particular situation.

Another helpful component in the building process that is available for many of the house plans in this book is a material list. A material list includes not only a detailed list of materials, but it also indicates where various cuts of lumber and other building components are to be used. This will save your general contractor significant time and money since they won't have to create this list before building begins. If a material list is available for a home, it is indicated on the home plans index on pages 134-135 in this book.

9 order materials

You can order materials yourself, or have your contractor do it. Nevertheless, in order to thoroughly enjoy your new home you will want to personally select many of the materials that go into its construction. Today, home improvement stores offer a wide variety of quality building products. Only you can decide what specific types of windows, cabinets, bath fixtures, etc. will make your new home yours. Spend time early on in the construction process looking at the materials and products available.

10 move in

With careful planning and organization, your new home will be built on schedule and ready for your move-in date. Be sure to have all of your important documents in place for the closing of your new home and then you'll be ready to move in and start living your dream.

Browse the pages of Waterfront Home Plans and discover over 180 home designs offered in a wide variety of sizes and styles and all with one thing in common – they are perfectly suited for a waterfront setting. Whether it's an expansive tranquil lake shore, or a narrow lively beach front, there's a home design here for anyone looking for their idyllic waterfront escape. Featuring amenities and features homeowners want in a Waterfront home today, these homes are designed to fit within your budget. So, let's begin your search for the perfect Waterfront home!

Top, left: Plan #F12-024D-0013 on page 16; top, right: Plan #F12-080D-0012 on page 53; Bottom, left: Plan #F12-056D-0120 on page 21 bottom, right: Plan #F12-170D-0003, on page 23.

The Perfect Home By The Water:
the must-have features right now

The sound of waves crashing in the distance, or the gentle sound of water splashing gently against the shoreline creates a sense of calmness unlike any other. Whichever sound beckons you to discover a life less stressed, seek that special place. The perfect home by the water captures the tranquility of its surroundings and allows you to experience a special feeling of inner peace from the moment you start your day there. Whether you're looking for a second dwelling, or you're interested in making a permanent move to a waterfront destination, there are some features that will make your waterfront home even more inviting, captivating and satisfying to your soul.

outside

Easy Access

Expansive decks, or comfortable outdoor living spaces that surround a home with additional areas to relax, entertain, and enjoy views are a must. Even better, make sure these outdoor areas are accessible from multiple areas of the home so enjoying the outdoors is effortless at any time. Add a door from the master suite to the deck and find yourself enjoying your morning coffee as the sun rises just steps from your bedroom. Or, create an entry near the kitchen and sunset happy hours and meals with friends will be easy. A covered deck is also a great outdoor retreat. Perfect for alfresco meals, it allows outdoor enjoyment without the intensity of direct sunlight, making it perfect for sunbelt regions, beach, or coastal homes with tropical heat and temperatures practically all year-round. Screen it in for a pest-free area that still allows breezes off the water to blow through. These types of spaces allow homeowners to feel unified with the outdoors and their waterfront surroundings and enjoy the convenience of being able to access the outdoor spaces freely from many areas of the home anytime.

Nightlite

Nothing is prettier than light reflecting off the water. Adding outdoor lighting around your property, on your deck, and even down the path to the boat dock to enhance the beauty of the lot as well as provide added security. Use lighting as a way to spotlight a special feature such as a unique rock garden, or water feature. Lighting also allows your home and boat dock to safely be seen from the water. And, when you're not home, it will deter people from entering your property. LED and solar powered lights make outdoor lighting easy to install, and more economical than ever before.

Keep It Clean

Whether it's been a long day burying the kids in the sand at the beach, or an afternoon of water skiing in the cool water of the lake, a welcomed addition to any waterfront home is an outdoor shower. Before anyone has a chance to step foot into your home, have them rinse off the day's fun in a handy outdoor shower and that also includes your furry friends, too. This feature will keep your home cleaner, free of debris, and will most likely extend the life of your floors.

Storage Galore

Everyone knows a home by the water will draw people to visit. These homes are inviting, offer many opportunities for making fun memories, provide a way for people to spend quality time outdoors, or just be more active. All of this fun can mean plenty of extra gear taking up lots of extra space. From skis and boogie boards to water floats and life preservers, these items are crucial components for outdoor fun, but require a great deal of space. Build a home design with an oversized garage, or consider adding a free-standing garage with plenty of storage, or consider even a stylish cabana to ensure all items have a have a "home" when not in use. When adding a garage, consider adding an additional garage bay, too. With frequent visitors, additional parking or entertaining space will be a nice addition.

Rustic, Cozy Touches

The use of stone and dark wood trim create a feeling of rustic charm if you build a rustic home near a lake or stream. Warm and cozy, family and guests will never want to leave their surroundings when decorated with these details. Or, build a stone fireplace that acts as a focal point in the main living space. Not only will it be beautiful, but it can provide an alternative heat source that will be sure to draw people in.

inside

Make Room For A Mud Room

Mud rooms are all the rage in home design right now, but add in the fact that you live near the water, and suddenly a mud room makes even more sense. With everyone playing in the water all day, shoes, clothing and beach bags are bound to come back to the house full of sand, dirt and most likely wet. Do yourself a favor and choose a design with a large mud room that features space for everyone's belongings to stay put when they're not coming and going. Create cubbies, lockers, or bins for everyone's personal items and have a large laundry area included or attached to capture all of those dirty clothes and wet swimsuits.

Light & Bright

Large dormer and picture windows make taking in views easy. Large windows offer compelling views, while still making the home feel like a private oasis tucked high above the shoreline. Pay attention to the rear elevation of the homes you like when building near the water. Chances are, you are going to want to capitalize on those beautiful views and will want as many windows across the back as possible. Make sure the main living spaces of your waterfront home have large, possibly two-story windows to enhance that water's edge feeling. In addition, well-lit bedrooms with oversized windows not only permit sunlight, but help stir waterfront breezes into the interior spaces. Keep in mind, the added sunlight can also help with the heating bills in the winter, but can make the home harder to keep cool in the summertime. Consider adding tint to the windows to shield the interior from too much sunlight and extra heat. Tinted windows also help keep your flooring, fabrics and furniture from fading due to the sunlight.

Standing Tall

Vaulted ceilings are a huge asset in most homes. Not only do they create a sense of spaciousness homes without vaulted ceilings lack, but they provide a way to add additional windows for enjoying the surrounding views. A two-story great room, for example, can enjoy twice as much view, while also including twice as many windows for added light inside the space. Vaulted or volume ceilings make a home feel larger than its true size and also create a light, airy feeling water's edge homes crave.

Be In Control

Home automation is taking home ownership by storm. With the help of apps downloaded onto your smart phone, a homeowner can now secure their home, turn on lights inside and out, turn down the thermostat, turn off an oven or even change the channel on the TV. So, adding home automation into your home design is a no-brainer, especially if your water's edge home is a second residence. The added security and efficiency provided by smart automation will give you peace of mind and keep money in your pocket.

Many of the features mentioned allow the natural beauty that surrounds your waterfront home to shine, while also providing additional function needed to keep your home looking its best. Whether it's a cozy stone fireplace surrounded in large windows showing off lake views, a shaded covered deck with comfortable seating, or an oversized mud room that keeps order amidst all the daily fun, these features will give your water's edge home a new level of function, comfort, and tranquility.

Plan #F12-101D-0124

Dimensions:	87'9" W x 73' D
Heated Sq. Ft.:	3,338
Bonus Sq. Ft.:	1,210
Bedrooms: 4	Bathrooms: 3½
Exterior Walls:	2" x 6"

Foundation: Basement, daylight basement or walk-out basement, please specify when ordering

See index for more information

Images provided by designer/architect

Features

- This floor plan features a second floor with two bedrooms that each have their own bath and walk-in closet plus there's a large loft area
- The first floor features a den/bedroom depending on your need, the well-appointed master suite, open gathering and dining spaces, and a luxury kitchen, great for entertaining
- The outdoor living spaces are ideal for backyard views thanks to multiple covered decks and a lower level covered patio
- The optional lower level has an additional 1,210 square feet of living area and a rec area with a bar, a bedroom, and a bath
- 2-car side entry garage, and a 1-car front entry garage

Second Floor
1,168 sq. ft.

© Copyright by
designer/architect

Optional Lower Level
1,210 sq. ft.

First Floor
2,170 sq. ft.

Plan #F12-032D-1142

Dimensions:	46' W x 32' D
Heated Sq. Ft.:	1,209
Bonus Sq. Ft.:	1,209
Bedrooms: 2	**Bathrooms: 1**
Exterior Walls:	2" x 6"

Foundation: Basement standard; crawl space, floating slab or monolithic slab for an additional fee

See index for more information

Features

- This stunning Modern home has an open-concept floor plan and gathering areas
- Two bedrooms are on the opposite side of the house from one another maintaining privacy
- The open kitchen has a large island with seating for four people to dine casually
- The living room has gorgeous views of the rear porch
- The optional lower level has an additional 1,209 square feet of living area

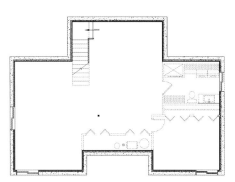

Optional
Lower Level
1,209 sq. ft.

First Floor
1,209 sq. ft.

© Copyright by
designer/architect

Images provided by designer/architect

Plan #F12-123D-0202

Dimensions: 64' W x 89' D
Heated Sq. Ft.: 1,856
Bonus Sq. Ft.: 1,032
Bedrooms: 2   **Bathrooms:** 2
Foundation: Walk-out basement standard; crawl space, slab or basement for an additional fee
See index for more information

Features

- This home was designed with perfect lake living in mind thanks to its wrap-around covered porch, huge covered patio, and screened deck area
- The huge vaulted beamed great room has a built-in fireplace and the kitchen on the opposite end with a long island for casual dining
- The private master bedroom has rear views and covered deck access, and a private bath
- A convenient guest suite on the first floor has direct access to a full bath
- The optional lower level has an additional 1,032 square feet of living area and includes a large family room with wet bar, a game table area, a handy half bath directly accessible from the outdoors, a bedroom, a bunk room, and a full bath
- 2-car side entry garage

Images provided by designer/architect

Optional Lower Level
1,032 sq. ft.

First Floor
1,856 sq. ft.

© Copyright by designer/architect

Second Floor
570 sq. ft.

© Copyright by designer/architect

Plan #F12-032D-0036

Dimensions:	30'8" W x 26' D
Heated Sq. Ft.:	1,285
Bedrooms: 2	Bathrooms: 2
Exterior Walls:	2" x 6"

Foundation: Basement standard; crawl space, floating slab or monolithic slab for an additional fee

See index for more information

Images provided by designer/architect

First Floor
715 sq. ft.

Second Floor
807 sq. ft.

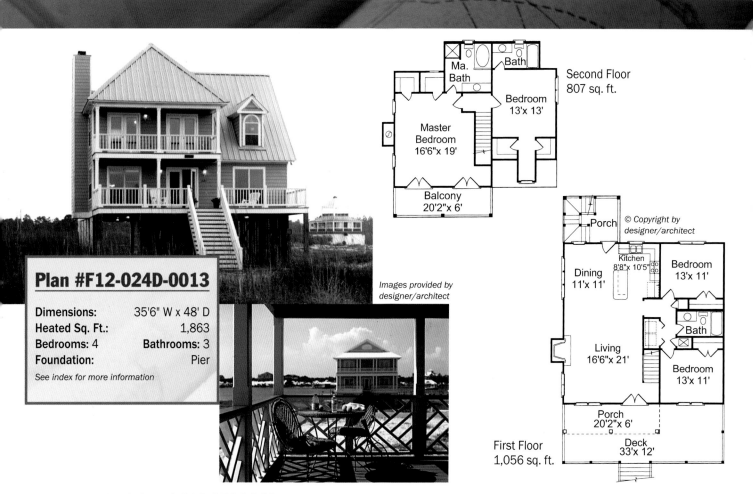

Plan #F12-024D-0013

Dimensions:	35'6" W x 48' D
Heated Sq. Ft.:	1,863
Bedrooms: 4	Bathrooms: 3
Foundation:	Pier

See index for more information

Images provided by designer/architect

© Copyright by designer/architect

First Floor
1,056 sq. ft.

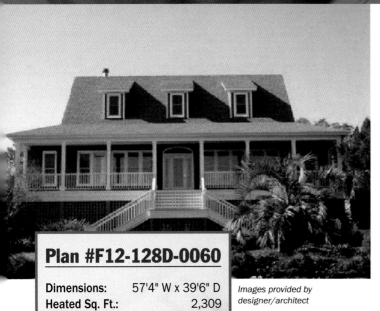

Plan #F12-128D-0060

Dimensions:	57'4" W x 39'6" D
Heated Sq. Ft.:	2,309
Bonus Sq. Ft.:	775
Bedrooms: 3	Bathrooms: 2½
Foundation:	Basement

See index for more information

Images provided by designer/architect

Second Floor
755 sq. ft.

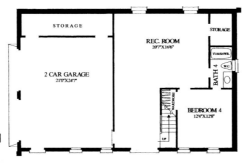

Optional Lower Level
775 sq. ft.

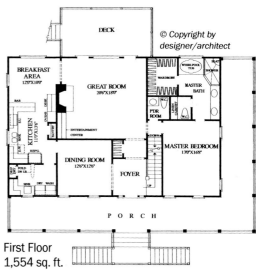

© Copyright by designer/architect

First Floor
1,554 sq. ft.

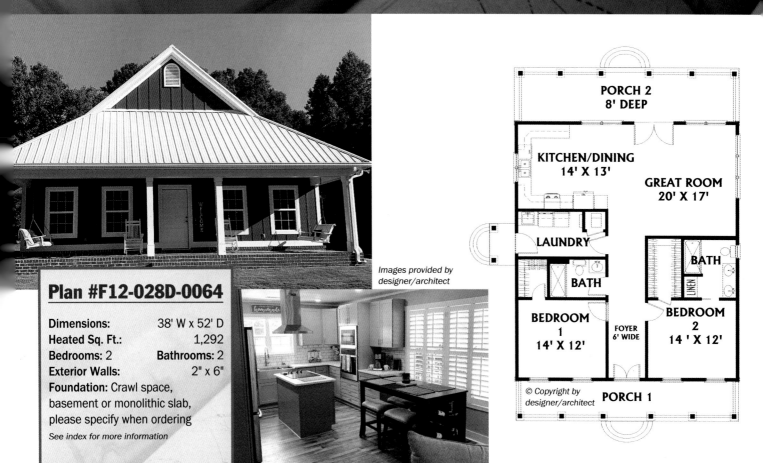

Plan #F12-028D-0064

Dimensions:	38' W x 52' D
Heated Sq. Ft.:	1,292
Bedrooms: 2	Bathrooms: 2
Exterior Walls:	2" x 6"

Foundation: Crawl space, basement or monolithic slab, please specify when ordering

See index for more information

Images provided by designer/architect

PORCH 2
8' DEEP

KITCHEN/DINING
14' X 13'

GREAT ROOM
20' X 17'

LAUNDRY

BATH

BATH

BEDROOM 1
14' X 12'

FOYER 6' WIDE

BEDROOM 2
14' X 12'

© Copyright by designer/architect

PORCH 1

Plan #F12-011D-0037

Dimensions:	40' W x 40' D
Heated Sq. Ft.:	2,262
Bedrooms: 3	Bathrooms: 2½
Exterior Walls:	2" x 6"
Foundation:	Slab

See index for more information

Images provided by designer/architect

Second Floor
960 sq. ft.

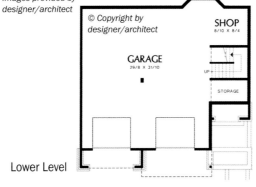

© Copyright by designer/architect

Lower Level

First Floor
1,302 sq. ft.

Plan #F12-032D-0553

Dimensions:	31'8" W x 24' D
Heated Sq. Ft.:	1,297
Bedrooms: 2	Bathrooms: 1½
Exterior Walls:	2" x 6"

Foundation: Basement standard; crawl space, floating slab or monolithic slab for an additional fee

See index for more information

Images provided by designer/architect

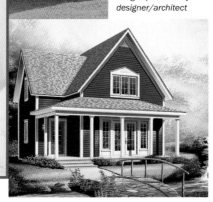

Second Floor
627 sq. ft.

© Copyright by designer/architect

First Floor
670 sq. ft.

18   call toll-free 1-800-373-2646   houseplansandmore.com

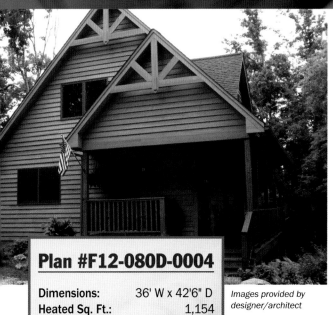

Plan #F12-080D-0004

Dimensions:	36' W x 42'6" D
Heated Sq. Ft.:	1,154
Bedrooms: 2	Bathrooms: 2
Exterior Walls:	2" x 6"
Foundation:	Crawl space

See index for more information

Images provided by designer/architect

© Copyright by designer/architect

First Floor
672 sq. ft.

Second Floor
482 sq. ft.

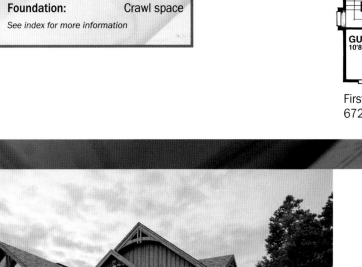

Plan #F12-101D-0119

Dimensions:	94'6" W x 113'1" D
Heated Sq. Ft.:	3,063
Bonus Sq. Ft.:	2,011
Bedrooms:	3
Bathrooms:	2 full, 2 half
Exterior Walls:	2" x 6"
Foundation: Basement, daylight basement or walk-out basement, please specify when ordering	

See index for more information

Images provided by designer/architect

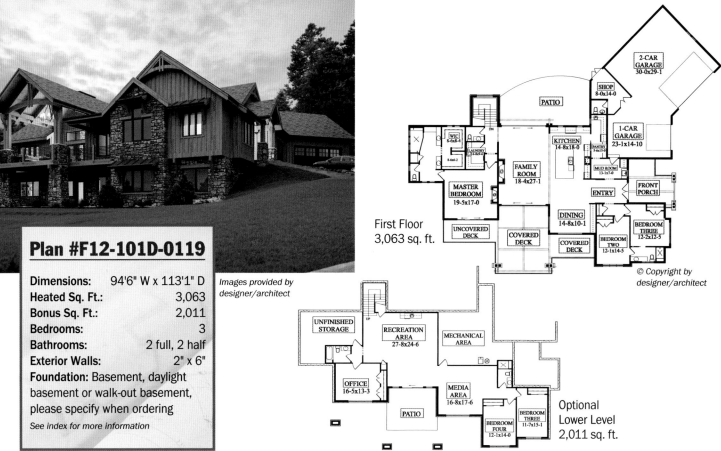

First Floor
3,063 sq. ft.

© Copyright by designer/architect

Optional
Lower Level
2,011 sq. ft.

Plan #F12-032D-0861

Dimensions:	28' W x 34' D
Heated Sq. Ft.:	1,301
Bedrooms: 3	**Bathrooms:** 2
Exterior Walls:	2" x 6"

Foundation: Walk-out basement standard; crawl space, floating slab or monolithic slab for an additional fee

See index for more information

Images provided by designer/architect

Second Floor
408 sq. ft.

First Floor
893 sq. ft.

© Copyright by designer/architect

Plan #F12-080D-0001

Dimensions:	24' W x 36' D
Heated Sq. Ft.:	583
Bedrooms: 1	**Bathrooms:** 1
Exterior Walls:	2" x 6"
Foundation:	Crawl space

See index for more information

Images provided by designer/architect

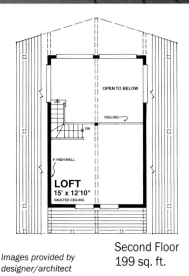

Second Floor
199 sq. ft.

© Copyright by designer/architect

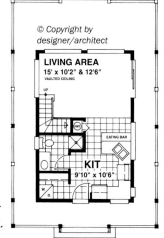

First Floor
384 sq. ft.

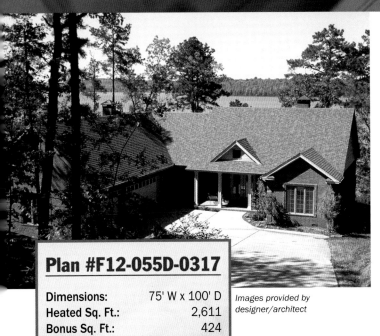

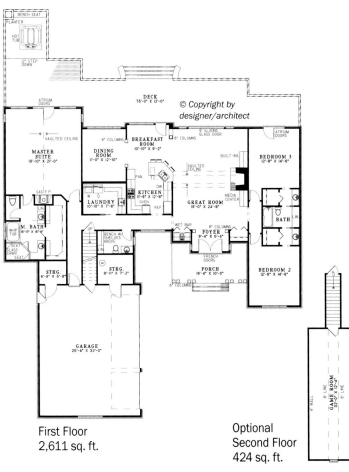

© Copyright by designer/architect

Plan #F12-055D-0317

Images provided by designer/architect

Dimensions:	75' W x 100' D
Heated Sq. Ft.:	2,611
Bonus Sq. Ft.:	424
Bedrooms: 3	Bathrooms: 2½
Foundation:	Daylight Basement

See index for more information

First Floor
2,611 sq. ft.

Optional
Second Floor
424 sq. ft.

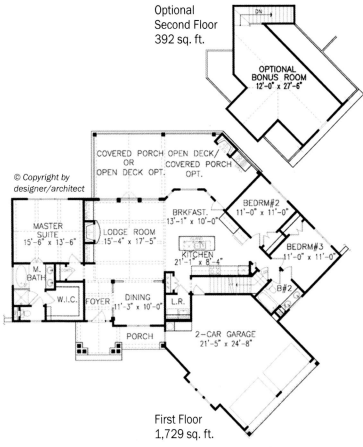

Optional
Second Floor
392 sq. ft.

© Copyright by
designer/architect

Plan #F12-056D-0120

Images provided by designer/architect

Dimensions:	74'6" W x 65' D
Heated Sq. Ft.:	1,729
Bonus Sq. Ft.:	392
Bedrooms: 3	Bathrooms: 2

Foundation: Basement standard;
crawl space or slab for an
additional fee

See index for more information

First Floor
1,729 sq. ft.

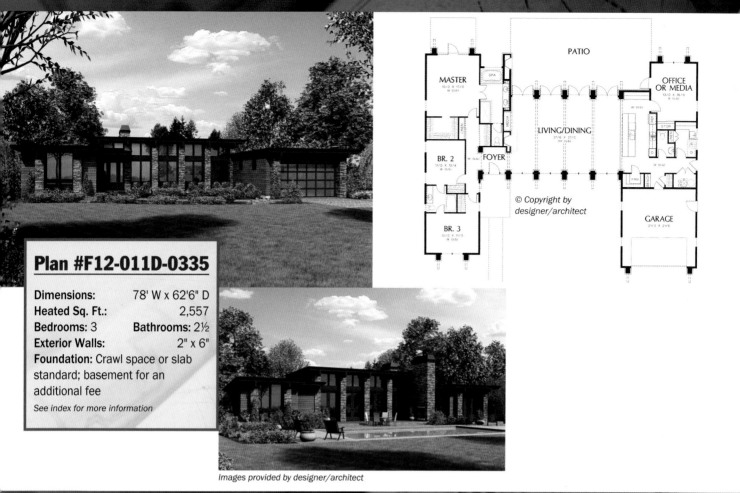

Plan #F12-011D-0335

Dimensions: 78' W x 62'6" D
Heated Sq. Ft.: 2,557
Bedrooms: 3   **Bathrooms:** 2½
Exterior Walls: 2" x 6"
Foundation: Crawl space or slab standard; basement for an additional fee

See index for more information

Images provided by designer/architect

Plan #F12-141D-0466

Dimensions: 48' W x 42'3" D
Heated Sq. Ft.: 3,288
Bedrooms: 3   **Bathrooms:** 2½
Foundation: Basement standard; crawl space, slab or walk-out basement for an additional fee

See index for more information

Images provided by designer/architect

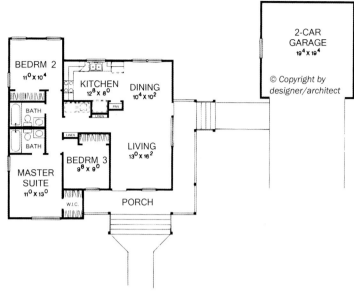

Plan #F12-111D-0032

Dimensions: 40' W x 37'6" D
Heated Sq. Ft.: 1,094
Bedrooms: 3   **Bathrooms:** 2
Foundation: Slab standard; crawl space or basement for an additional fee

See index for more information

Images provided by designer/architect

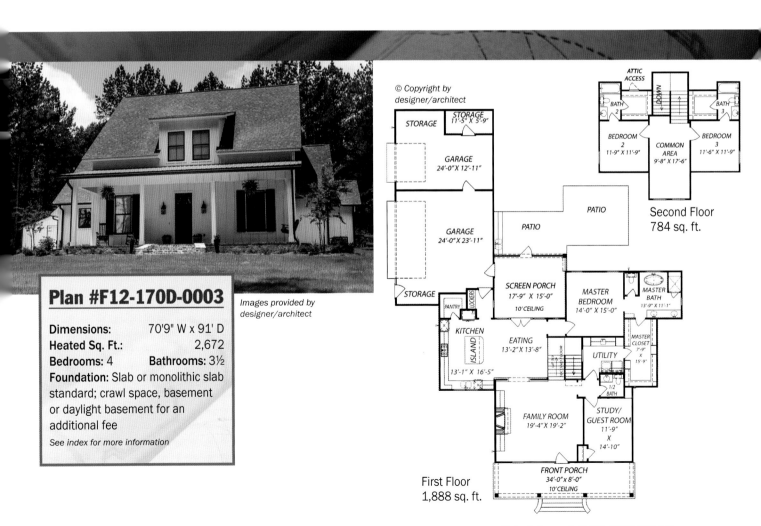

Plan #F12-170D-0003

Dimensions: 70'9" W x 91' D
Heated Sq. Ft.: 2,672
Bedrooms: 4   **Bathrooms:** 3½
Foundation: Slab or monolithic slab standard; crawl space, basement or daylight basement for an additional fee

See index for more information

Images provided by designer/architect

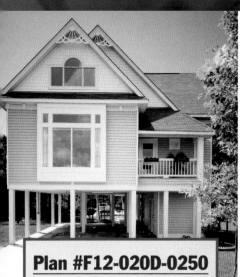

Plan #F12-020D-0250

Dimensions:	34' W x 52' D
Heated Sq. Ft.:	2,020
Bedrooms: 4	Bathrooms: 3
Exterior Walls:	2" x 6"
Foundation:	Pier

See index for more information

Images provided by designer/architect

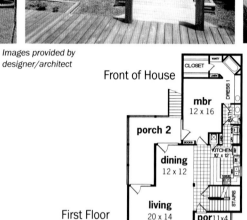

Front of House

mbr
12 x 16

porch 2

dining
12 x 12

living
20 x 14

First Floor
1,182 sq. ft.

© Copyright by designer/architect

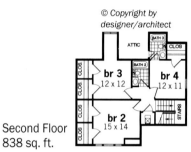

ATTIC

br 3
12 x 12

br 4
12 x 11

br 2
15 x 14

Second Floor
838 sq. ft.

Plan #F12-024D-0312

Dimensions:	49' W x 62' D
Heated Sq. Ft.:	1,936
Bonus Sq. Ft.:	448
Bedrooms: 4	Bathrooms: 2
Foundation:	Pier

See index for more information

Images provided by designer/architect

Optional
Second Floor
448 sq. ft.

Open to Below

Unfinished Gameroom
16'9"x 18'11"

Shelf

© Copyright by designer/architect

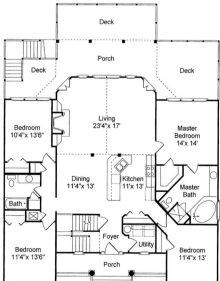

Deck

Porch

Deck

Deck

Bedroom
10'4"x 13'6"

Living
23'4"x 17'

Master Bedroom
14'x 14'

Dining
11'4"x 13'

Kitchen
11'x 13'

Master Bath

Bath

Bedroom
11'4"x 13'6"

Foyer

Utility

Bedroom
11'4"x 13'

Porch

First Floor
1,936 sq. ft.

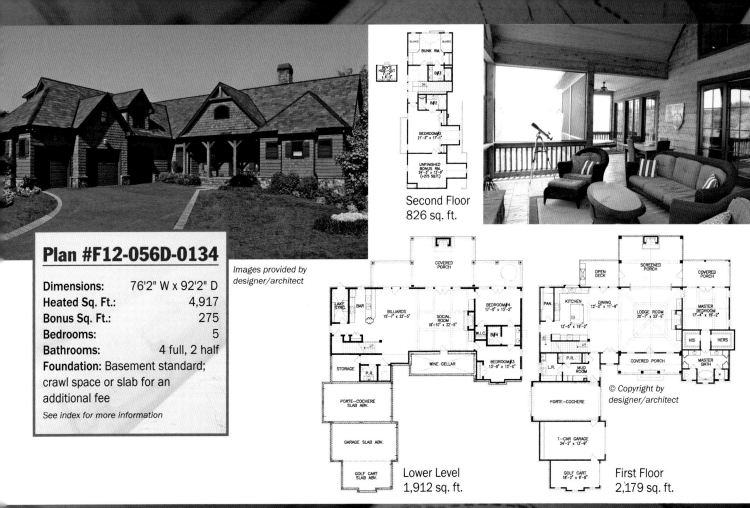

Second Floor
826 sq. ft.

Plan #F12-056D-0134

Dimensions:	76'2" W x 92'2" D
Heated Sq. Ft.:	4,917
Bonus Sq. Ft.:	275
Bedrooms:	5
Bathrooms:	4 full, 2 half

Foundation: Basement standard; crawl space or slab for an additional fee

See index for more information

Images provided by designer/architect

© Copyright by designer/architect

Lower Level
1,912 sq. ft.

First Floor
2,179 sq. ft.

Plan #F12-026D-2011

Dimensions:	40' W x 50'8" D
Heated Sq. Ft.:	1,750
Bedrooms: 3	**Bathrooms:** 2½
Exterior Walls:	2" x 6"

Foundation: Basement standard; crawl space, slab or walk-out basement for an additional fee

See index for more information

Images provided by designer/architect

© Copyright by designer/architect

Owner's Suite
13⁰ x 14³

Br.2
10⁰ x 10⁶

Br.3
11³ x 11³

Second Floor
823 sq. ft.

First Floor
927 sq. ft.

Plan #F12-024D-0813

Dimensions:	36' W x 68' D
Heated Sq. Ft.:	1,728
Bedrooms: 3	Bathrooms: 3
Foundation:	Pilings

See index for more information

Features

- This raised one-story home is ideal for coastal regions and offers parking underneath the home
- The kitchen overlooks both the dining and living areas for added openness
- The private master bedroom has covered porch access, a walk-in closet, and a private bath with a free-standing tub as well as a walk-in shower
- An oversized elevator makes reaching the home easy and highly accessible for all physical abilities from the parking area underneath

© Copyright by designer/architect

Images provided by designer/architect

Plan #F12-101D-0142

Dimensions:	72' W x 82'6" D
Heated Sq. Ft.:	2,700
Bonus Sq. Ft.:	1,991
Bedrooms: 2	Bathrooms: 2½
Exterior Walls:	2" x 6"
Foundation:	Walk-out basement

See index for more information

Images provided by designer/architect

© Copyright by designer/architect

Optional Lower Level 1,991 sq. ft.

First Floor 2,700 sq. ft.

Second Floor 485 sq. ft.

First Floor 1,356 sq. ft.

Plan #F12-141D-0084

Dimensions:	38'2" W x 44'6" D
Heated Sq. Ft.:	1,841
Bedrooms: 3	Bathrooms: 2½
Exterior Walls:	2" x 6"

Foundation: Partial crawl space/ slab standard; slab, basement or walk-out basement for an additional fee

See index for more information

Images provided by designer/architect

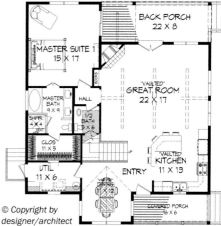

© Copyright by designer/architect

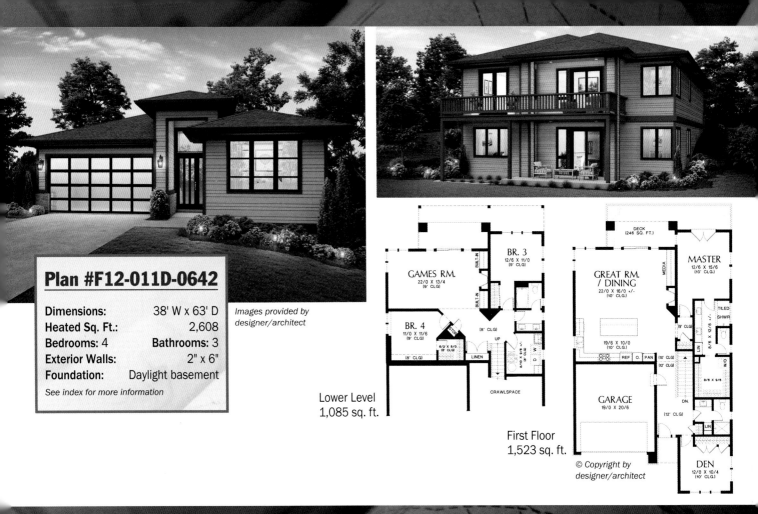

Plan #F12-011D-0642

Dimensions:	38' W x 63' D
Heated Sq. Ft.:	2,608
Bedrooms: 4	Bathrooms: 3
Exterior Walls:	2" x 6"
Foundation:	Daylight basement

See index for more information

Images provided by designer/architect

Lower Level
1,085 sq. ft.

GAMES RM.
22/0 X 13/4
(9' CLG)

BR. 4
11/0 X 11/6
(9' CLG)

BR. 3
12/6 X 11/0
(9' CLG)

CRAWLSPACE

First Floor
1,523 sq. ft.

GREAT RM. / DINING
22/0 X 16/0 +/-
(10' CLG)

MASTER
12/6 X 15/6
(10' CLG)

DECK
(246 SQ. FT.)

GARAGE
19/0 X 20/6

DEN
12/0 X 10/4
(10' CLG)

© Copyright by designer/architect

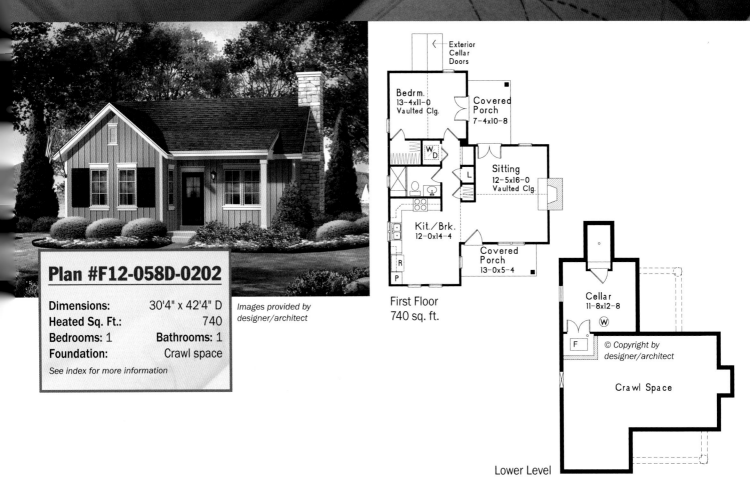

Plan #F12-058D-0202

Dimensions:	30'4" x 42'4" D
Heated Sq. Ft.:	740
Bedrooms: 1	Bathrooms: 1
Foundation:	Crawl space

See index for more information

Images provided by designer/architect

Exterior Cellar Doors

Bedrm.
13-4x11-0
Vaulted Clg.

Covered Porch
7-4x10-8

Sitting
12-5x16-0
Vaulted Clg.

Kit./Brk.
12-0x14-4

Covered Porch
13-0x5-4

First Floor
740 sq. ft.

Cellar
11-8x12-8

© Copyright by designer/architect

Crawl Space

Lower Level

Plan #F12-111D-0051

Dimensions: 33' W x 57' D
Heated Sq. Ft.: 2,346
Bedrooms: 2   **Bathrooms:** 3½
Foundation: Slab standard; crawl space or basement for an additional fee

See index for more information

Images provided by designer/architect

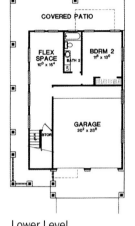

Second Floor
594 sq. ft.

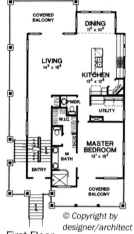

Lower Level
624 sq. ft.

First Floor
1,128 sq. ft.

© Copyright by designer/architect

Plan #F12-141D-0051

Dimensions: 33'4" W x 59'3" D
Heated Sq. Ft.: 2,000
Bedrooms: 4   **Bathrooms:** 4
Foundation: Pier standard; crawl space, slab, basement or walk-out basement for an additional fee

See index for more information

Images provided by designer/architect

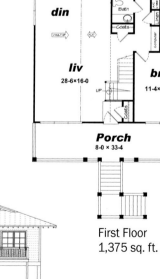

© Copyright by designer/architect

First Floor
1,375 sq. ft.

Second Floor
625 sq. ft.

Rear View

First Floor
1,217 sq. ft.

WALK-IN
4'-0" X 5'-8"

WALK-IN
7'-10" X 5'-8"

BEDROOM #2
10'-0" X 11'-0"

BATHROOM
8'-10" X 5'-10"

LINEN

MASTER BEDROOM
14'-0" X 12'-0"

DOWN

REF

KITCHEN
14'-0" X 12'-8"

BALCONY
12'-0" X 30'-0"

LIVING ROOM
15'-0" X 13'-6"

CATHEDRAL CEILING

DINING ROOM
14'-0" X 13'-8"

Plan #F12-148D-0048

Dimensions:	44' W x 30' D
Heated Sq. Ft.:	1,217
Bonus Sq. Ft.:	1,217
Bedrooms: 2	**Bathrooms:** 1
Exterior Walls:	2" x 6"
Foundation:	Walk-out basement

See index for more information

Images provided by designer/architect

Optional Lower Level
1,217 sq. ft.

STORAGE
14'-2" X 6'-0"

BATHROOM
10'-0" X 8'-2"

BEDROOM #4
10'-6" X 10'-4"

PLAYING ROOM
14'-2" X 17'-8"

STORAGE

FAMILY ROOM
13'-4" X 13'-2"

BEDROOM #3
14'-2" X 11'-0"

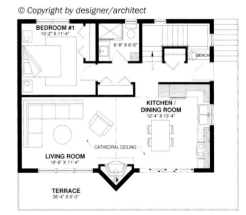

BEDROOM #1
10'-2" X 11'-4"

6'-8" X 6'-0"

BENCH

KITCHEN / DINING ROOM
12'-4" X 13'-4"

LIVING ROOM
18'-8" X 11'-4"

CATHEDRAL CEILING

TERRACE
36'-4" X 6'-0"

First Floor
787 sq. ft.

Plan #F12-032D-0032

Dimensions:	32'4" W x 24'4" D
Heated Sq. Ft.:	1,574
Bedrooms: 3	**Bathrooms:** 2
Exterior Walls:	2" x 6"
Foundation:	Walk-out basement

See index for more information

Images provided by designer/architect

BEDROOM #2
11'-6" X 10'-4"

STACKED WASHER DRYER

BEDROOM #3
13'-2" X 9'-4"

WOOD STOVE

FAMILY ROOM
16'-10" X 15'-4"

Lower Level
787 sq. ft.

Plan #F12-101D-0155

Dimensions:	34' W x 28' D
Heated Sq. Ft.:	952
Bedrooms: 1	Bathrooms: 1
Exterior Walls:	2" x 6"
Foundation:	Slab

See index for more information

Features

- This Modern dwelling may be smaller in size, but it makes up for its small footprint with great style and function
- Enter from the covered deck and find an entirely open living area with fireplace that connects to the open dining area and kitchen
- The kitchen features a huge window above the sink extending the interior into the outdoor surroundings perfectly and filling the interior with sunlight from every direction
- The dining area is also sun-filled with multiple windows filling the space with natural light
- The bedroom has two corner closets and is only steps from the bathroom
- A home office with a large walk-in closet right outside its door is a nice place to quietly get work done

Images provided by designer/architect

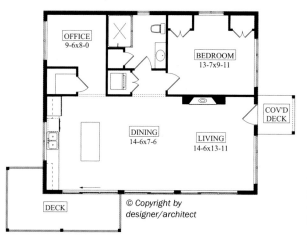

OFFICE
9-6x8-0

BEDROOM
13-7x9-11

COV'D DECK

DINING
14-6x7-6

LIVING
14-6x13-11

DECK

© Copyright by designer/architect

Plan #F12-032D-1110

Dimensions:	64' W x 49' D
Heated Sq. Ft.:	1,704
Bonus Sq. Ft.:	1,704
Bedrooms: 3	Bathrooms: 2
Exterior Walls:	2" x 6"

Foundation: Basement standard; crawl space, floating slab or monolithic slab for an additional fee

See index for more information

Images provided by designer/architect

© Copyright by designer/architect

Features

- Modern style and simplicity provide the perfect home for that tranquil waterfront setting
- The front foyer has great function with storage and a built-in bench
- A laundry room with a barn style door is to the left, while two bedrooms and a full bath are to the right
- The master suite is located in its own hall with a walk-in closet and a luxurious spa style bath
- The kitchen has a huge island surrounded in storage
- The dining and living rooms combine and enjoy the view of the fireplace flanked by windows
- The optional lower level has an additional 1,704 square feet of living area
- 2-car front entry garage

First Floor
1,704 sq. ft.

Optional
Lower Level
1,704 sq. ft.

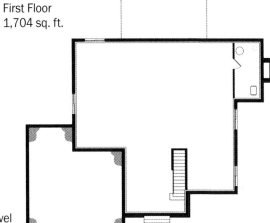

Plan #F12-126D-1175

Dimensions:	28' W x 26' D
Heated Sq. Ft.:	910
Bedrooms: 2	**Bathrooms:** 1½
Exterior Walls:	2" x 6"
Foundation:	Slab

See index for more information

Images provided by designer/architect

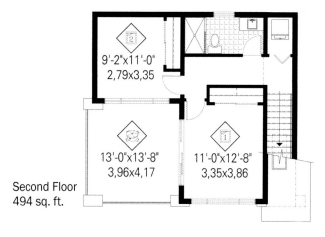

9'-2"x11'-0"
2,79x3,35

13'-0"x13'-8"
3,96x4,17

11'-0"x12'-8"
3,35x3,86

Second Floor
494 sq. ft.

© Copyright by designer/architect

11'-0''x12'-6''
3,35x3,81

11'-6''x24'-6''
3,51x7,47

11'-0''x12'-0''
3,35x3,66

First Floor
416 sq. ft.

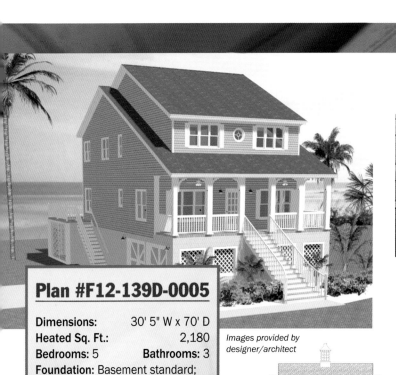

Plan #F12-139D-0005

Dimensions:	30' 5" W x 70' D
Heated Sq. Ft.:	2,180
Bedrooms: 5	**Bathrooms:** 3

Foundation: Basement standard; crawl space, slab, daylight basement or walk-out basement for an additional fee

See index for more information

Images provided by designer/architect

Rear View

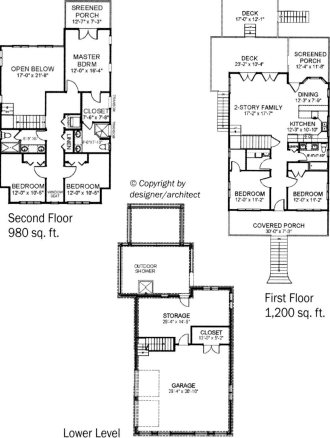

SCREENED PORCH
12'-7" x 7'-3"

OPEN BELOW
17'-0" x 21'-8"

MASTER BDRM
12'-0" x 16'-4"

CLOSET
7'-6" x 7'-8"

LINEN

BEDROOM
12'-0" x 10'-5"

BEDROOM
12'-0" x 10'-5"

WINDOW SEAT

Second Floor
980 sq. ft.

DECK
17'-0" x 12'-1"

DECK
23'-2" x 10'-4"

SCREENED PORCH
12'-4" x 11'-8"

2-STORY FAMILY
17'-2" x 17'-7"

DINING
12'-3" x 7'-9"

KITCHEN
12'-3" x 10'-10"

BEDROOM
12'-0" x 11'-2"

BEDROOM
12'-0" x 11'-2"

COVERED PORCH
30'-0" x 7'-3"

First Floor
1,200 sq. ft.

© Copyright by designer/architect

OUTDOOR SHOWER

STORAGE
29'-4" x 14'-5"

CLOSET
12'-0" x 5'-2"

GARAGE
29'-4" x 26'-10"

Lower Level

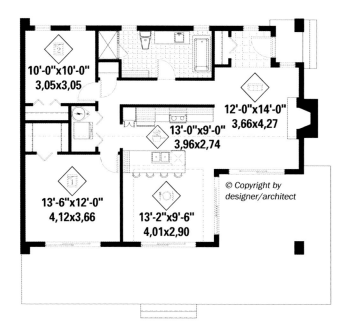

Plan #F12-126D-1151

Dimensions:	40' W x 30' D
Heated Sq. Ft.:	1,060
Bedrooms: 2	Bathrooms: 1
Exterior Walls:	2" x 6"
Foundation:	Crawl space

See index for more information

Images provided by designer/architect

10'-0"x10'-0"
3,05x3,05

12'-0"x14'-0"
3,66x4,27

13'-0"x9'-0"
3,96x2,74

13'-6"x12'-0"
4,12x3,66

13'-2"x9'-6"
4,01x2,90

© Copyright by designer/architect

Plan #F12-013D-0243

Dimensions:	28' W x 26' D
Heated Sq. Ft.:	514
Bedrooms: 1	Bathrooms: 1
Exterior Walls:	2" x 6"

Foundation: Slab standard; crawl space or basement for an additional fee

See index for more information

Images provided by designer/architect

COVERED PORCH
27'-4" X 7'-7"

EAT-IN KITCHEN
13' X 17'

BATH
8'-3" X 5'-0"

CLOSET
5'-0" X 5'-0"

PANTRY

LIVING

BEDROOM
13'-8" X 11'-8"

COVERED PORCH
14'-0" X 6'-0"

© Copyright by designer/architect

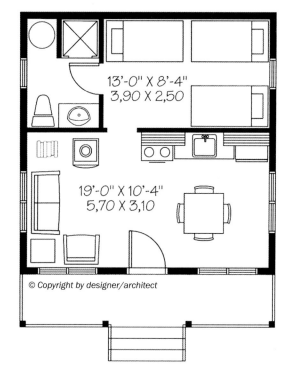

13'-0" X 8'-4"
3,90 X 2,50

19'-0" X 10'-4"
5,70 X 3,10

© Copyright by designer/architect

Plan #F12-032D-0708

Dimensions:	20' W x 20' D
Heated Sq. Ft.:	400
Bedrooms: 1	**Bathrooms:** 1
Exterior Walls:	2" x 6"

Foundation: Screw pile standard; crawl space, floating slab or monolithic slab for an additional fee

See index for more information

Images provided by designer/architect

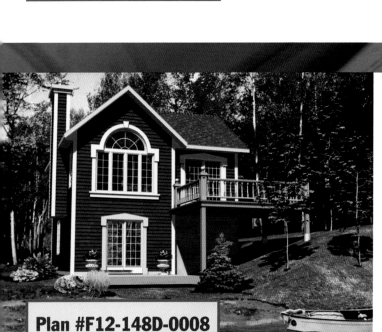

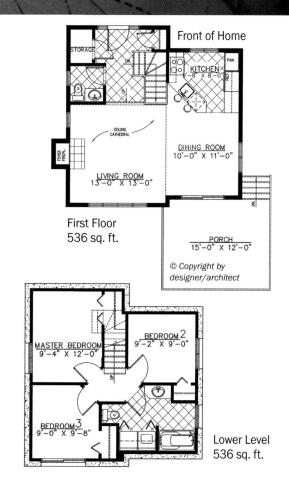

Front of Home

STORAGE

KITCHEN
9'-8" X 8'-0"

PAN.

CEILING CATHEDRAL

DINING ROOM
10'-0" X 11'-0"

FOYER

LIVING ROOM
13'-0" X 13'-0"

DN

First Floor
536 sq. ft.

PORCH
15'-0" X 12'-0"

© Copyright by designer/architect

MASTER BEDROOM
9'-4" X 12'-0"

BEDROOM 2
9'-2" X 9'-0"

BEDROOM 3
9'-0" X 9'-8"

Lower Level
536 sq. ft.

Plan #F12-148D-0008

Dimensions:	24' W x 24' D
Heated Sq. Ft.:	1,072
Bedrooms: 3	**Bathrooms:** 1½
Exterior Walls:	2" x 6"
Foundation:	Walk-out basement

See index for more information

Images provided by designer/architect

Front View

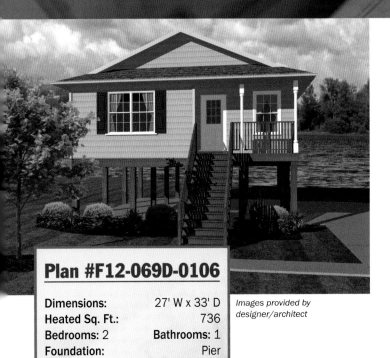

Plan #F12-069D-0106

Dimensions: 27' W x 33' D
Heated Sq. Ft.: 736
Bedrooms: 2 Bathrooms: 1
Foundation: Pier

See index for more information

Images provided by designer/architect

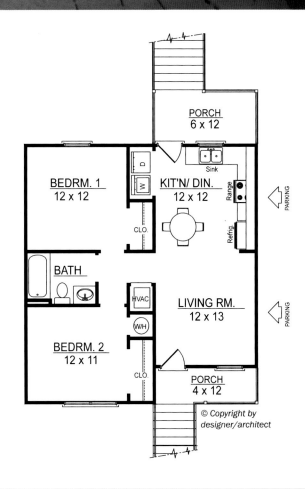

PORCH
6 x 12

BEDRM. 1
12 x 12

KIT'N/ DIN.
12 x 12

Sink

D

W

CLO.

BATH

HVAC

W/H

LIVING RM.
12 x 13

BEDRM. 2
12 x 11

CLO.

PORCH
4 x 12

Range

Refrig.

PARKING

PARKING

© Copyright by designer/architect

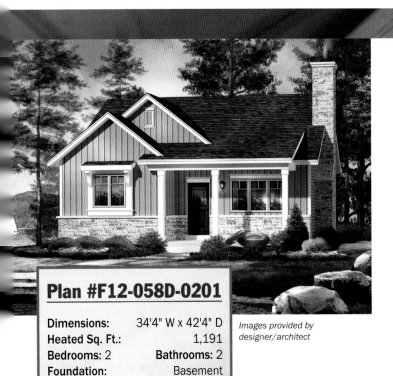

Plan #F12-058D-0201

Dimensions: 34'4" W x 42'4" D
Heated Sq. Ft.: 1,191
Bedrooms: 2 Bathrooms: 2
Foundation: Basement

See index for more information

Images provided by designer/architect

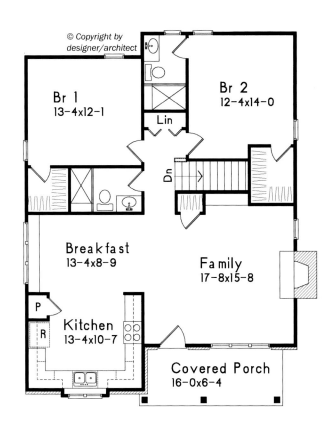

© Copyright by designer/architect

Br 1
13-4x12-1

Br 2
12-4x14-0

Lin

Dn

Breakfast
13-4x8-9

Family
17-8x15-8

P

R

Kitchen
13-4x10-7

Covered Porch
16-0x6-4

Plan #F12-076D-0220

Dimensions:	97'2" W x 87'7" D
Heated Sq. Ft.:	3,061
Bonus Sq. Ft.:	3,644
Bedrooms: 3	**Bathrooms** 3½

Foundation: Basement standard; crawl space or slab for an additional fee

See index for more information

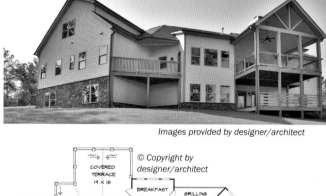

Images provided by designer/architect

Features

- This luxury Craftsman home is loaded with curb appeal thanks to multiple gables, and a covered porch adding that undeniable charm
- The first floor is open and airy with the main gathering spaces combining perfectly maximizing the square footage
- The kitchen is open to the family room with a grilling terrace nearby
- The optional lower level has an additional 2,975 square feet of living area including a hobby room, theater, office, and a recreation area with a bar
- The optional second floor has an additional 669 square feet of living area with 277 square feet in the bedroom and 392 square feet in the recreation area
- 3-car front entry garage

© Copyright by designer/architect

Optional
Lower Level
2,975 sq. ft.

First Floor
3,061 sq. ft.

Optional
Second Floor
669 sq. ft.

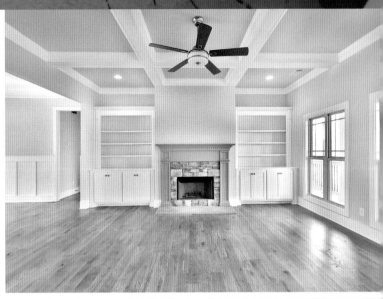

Plan #F12-091D-0506

Dimensions:	82' W x 71' D
Heated Sq. Ft.:	2,241
Bonus Sq. Ft.:	591
Bedrooms: 3	Bathrooms: 2½
Exterior Walls:	2" x 6"

Foundation: Crawl space standard; slab, basement or walk-out basement for an additional fee

See index for more information

Features

- Quaint cottage style creates an inviting exterior with tons of curb appeal
- The L-shaped covered front porch is a friendly feature and creates plenty of space for relaxing in the shade
- Vaulted front to back, step into this home and discover a spacious great room that leads to an open dining room and beyond to a kitchen with a huge 9' long island
- The master suite is separated from the other bedrooms for privacy
- A handy rear entry is perfect when friends come over
- The optional bonus room on the second floor has an additional 591 square feet of living area
- 2-car front entry garage

First Floor
2,241 sq. ft.

Optional
Second Floor
591 sq. ft.

Plan #F12-056D-0141

Dimensions:	70'7" W x 52'4" D
Heated Sq. Ft.:	2,510
Bonus Sq. Ft.:	371
Bedrooms: 4	Bathrooms: 3

Foundation: Basement standard; crawl space or slab for an additional fee

See index for more information

Images provided by designer/architect

Features

- Classic Craftsman style on the outside with extra rustic touches on the inside makes this home extra welcoming upon arrival
- The open kitchen with island looks out over the lake room and beyond to views of the deck
- The vaulted master bedroom enjoys direct access onto the screened porch with a cozy outdoor fireplace
- The lake room also has a cozy fireplace and enjoys great views of the lake from a huge window wall
- The lower level has an optional social room with an additional 371 square feet of living area
- 2-car front entry garage

© Copyright by designer/architect

First Floor
1,718 sq. ft.

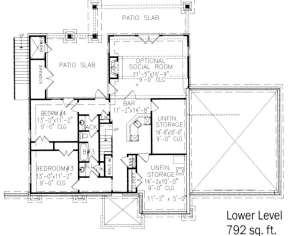

Lower Level
792 sq. ft.

Optional Second Floor 1,769 sq. ft.

BALCONY 10'-0" x 4'-7"

BEDROOM 5 10'-0" x 12'-0"

SITTING 12'-11" x 12'-0"

COMPUTER CENTER 14'-10" x 12'-1"

RECREATION AREA 25'-10" x 27'-4"

BEDROOM 4 18'-11" x 12'-1"

BONUS AREA 10'-0" x 25'-6"

Images provided by designer/architect

First Floor 1,975 sq. ft.

MASTER SUITE 21'-2" x 16'-3"

SITTING

DECK 49'-0" x 9'-7"

BEDROOM 2 13'-7" x 11'-0"

SCREENED PORCH 15'-1" x 11'-7"

EAT-IN KITCHEN 14'-3" x 22'-6"

OPTIONAL EXTERIOR BATH ACCESS

RV TOY STORAGE

LAUNDRY

FAMILY ROOM 28'-8" x 21'-0"

BEDROOM 3 13'-2" x 11'-0"

GARAGE 21'-2" x 34'-0"

PORCH 29'-4" x 6'-0"

© Copyright by designer/architect

Plan #F12-013D-0181

Dimensions:	71'2" W x 64'6" D
Heated Sq. Ft.:	1,975
Bonus Sq. Ft.:	1,769
Bedrooms: 3	**Bathrooms:** 3½

Foundation: Crawl space standard; basement or slab for an additional fee

See index for more information

BEDROOM 1 13' x 12'

LAUNDRY

BEDROOM 2 12' x 10'

BATH

DINING AREA 10' x 6'

GREAT ROOM 18' x 14'

KITCHEN 13' x 13'

PANTRY

© Copyright by designer/architect

8' WIDE COVERED PORCH

Images provided by designer/architect

Plan #F12-028D-0090

Dimensions:	31' W x 40' D
Heated Sq. Ft.:	992
Bedrooms: 2	**Bathrooms:** 1
Exterior Walls:	2" x 6"

Foundation: Slab or crawl space, please specify when ordering

See index for more information

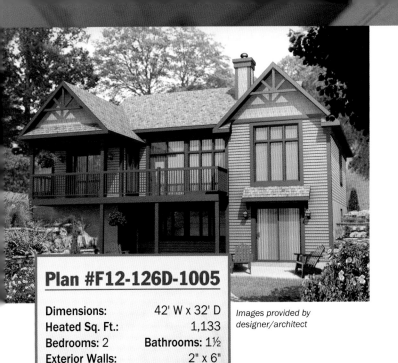

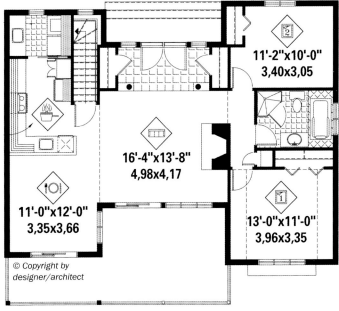

Plan #F12-126D-1005

Dimensions:	42' W x 32' D
Heated Sq. Ft.:	1,133
Bedrooms: 2	Bathrooms: 1½
Exterior Walls:	2" x 6"
Foundation:	Basement

See index for more information

Images provided by designer/architect

© Copyright by designer/architect

11'-2"x10'-0"
3,40x3,05

16'-4"x13'-8"
4,98x4,17

11'-0"x12'-0"
3,35x3,66

13'-0"x11'-0"
3,96x3,35

Plan #F12-013D-0231

Dimensions:	44'1" W x 62' D
Heated Sq. Ft.:	1,604
Bonus Sq. Ft.:	295
Bedrooms: 2	Bathrooms: 2
Foundation:	Basement

See index for more information

Images provided by designer/architect

DECK
12'-7" x 7'-7"

SUITE 1
16'-0" x 12'-0"

OPEN BELOW

Second Floor
316 sq. ft.

MECH.

SUITE 3
11'-3" x 11'-11"

CLOSET
6'-6" x 7'-8"

OPTIONAL
DRIVE-UNDER
GARAGE
26'-11" x 29'-1"

**Optional
Lower Level**
295 sq. ft.

First Floor
1,288 sq. ft.

DECK

SUITE 2
13'-9" x 10'-0"

MULTI-
PURPOSE
ROOM
11'-4" x 9'-0"

KITCHEN
11'-11" x 9'-10"

GREAT ROOM
27'-4" x 29'-5"

COVERED PORCH
24'-4" x 7'-7"

© Copyright by designer/architect

Plan #F12-141D-0061

Dimensions:	46' W x 46' D
Heated Sq. Ft.:	1,273
Bedrooms: 2	**Bathrooms:** 2

Foundation: Crawl space standard; slab, basement or walk-out basement for an additional fee

See index for more information

Features

- Quite possibly the perfect layout for a vacation getaway, or an empty nester home with private space for guests and the homeowners
- The vaulted country kitchen merges completely with the great room to form the core of this open and airy layout
- The master bedroom has plenty of space to relax in private and enjoys direct deck access, a posh bath and a huge walk-in closet
- Bedroom 2 has direct screen porch access and is right across the hall from a full bath and the laundry room
- So much outdoor living space surrounds this home it's easy to see why it would be the ideal home for a lake or waterfront setting

Images provided by designer/architect

Plan #F12-024D-0008

Dimensions: 36'6" W x 47'5" D
Heated Sq. Ft.: 1,650
Bedrooms: 4   **Bathrooms:** 2
Foundation: Pilings or slab, please specify when ordering

See index for more information

Features

- The wide open living area connects to a charming dining area and enjoys access to both the front porch as well as the rear porch

- This two-story living area features lots of windows for views to the outdoors and a large fireplace for a warm, inviting atmosphere indoors

- An efficiently designed kitchen enjoys an island for plenty of counterspace

- The master bedroom is located on the second floor for privacy

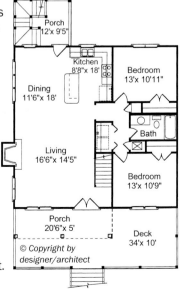

First Floor
1,122 sq. ft.

© Copyright by designer/architect

Second Floor
528 sq. ft.

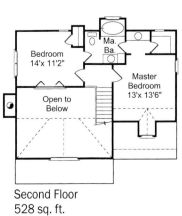

Images provided by designer/architect

Plan #F12-141D-0460

Dimensions:	74'6" W x 38' D
Heated Sq. Ft.:	2,650
Bedrooms: 3	**Bathrooms:** 2½
Exterior Walls:	2" x 6"

Foundation: Slab standard; crawl space, basement or walk-out basement for an additional fee

See index for more information

Images provided by designer/architect

Second Floor
1,172 sq. ft.

First Floor
1,478 sq. ft.

© Copyright by designer/architect

Plan #F12-007D-0244

Dimensions:	59' W x 52' D
Heated Sq. Ft.:	1,605
Bedrooms: 2	**Bathrooms:** 2
Foundation:	Walk-out basement

See index for more information

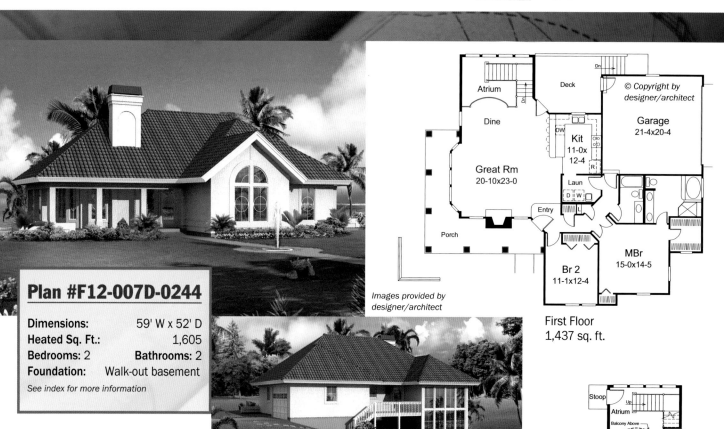

Images provided by designer/architect

First Floor
1,437 sq. ft.

Lower Level
168 sq. ft.

Plan #F12-028D-0109

Dimensions:	33' W x 40' D
Heated Sq. Ft.:	890
Bedrooms: 2	Bathrooms: 1
Exterior Walls:	2" x 6"
Foundation:	Crawl space or slab, please specify when ordering

See index for more information

Images provided by designer/architect

PORCH 8'-0" DEEP

LAUNDRY 7-3 X 6-6

BEDROOM 2 14-0 X 10-0

BATH 7-0 X 10-0

KITCHEN 12-0 X 11-6

BEDROOM 1 13-0 X 10-0

GREAT ROOM 20-0 X 14-0

PORCH 8'-0" DEEP

© Copyright by designer/architect

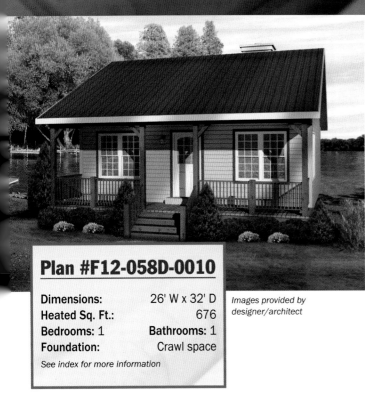

Plan #F12-058D-0010

Dimensions:	26' W x 32' D
Heated Sq. Ft.:	676
Bedrooms: 1	Bathrooms: 1
Foundation:	Crawl space

See index for more information

Images provided by designer/architect

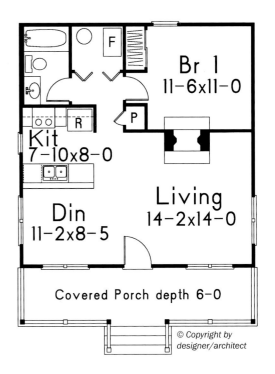

Br 1 11-6x11-0

Kit 7-10x8-0

Din 11-2x8-5

Living 14-2x14-0

Covered Porch depth 6-0

© Copyright by designer/architect

Detached Garage
23-4x23-4

© Copyright by
designer/architect

Images provided by
designer/architect

(Floor plan labels: Patio, MBr 13-8x15-0 Std Coffer Opt Vault, Dining/Brkfst 13-6x13-4 Vaulted, Kit 10-7x 13-4 Vaulted, Br 2 10-0x10-6, Great Rm 17-8x17-8 Vaulted, Entry, Br 3 13-8x11-8, Porch)

Plan #F12-121D-0016

Dimensions:	42'4" W x 54' D
Heated Sq. Ft.:	1,582
Bedrooms: 3	**Bathrooms:** 2

Foundation: Basement standard; crawl space or slab for an additional fee

See index for more information

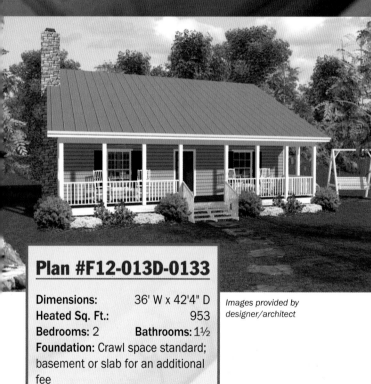

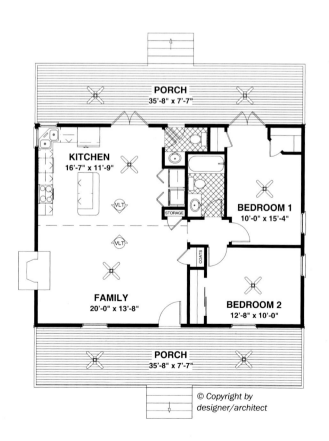

(Floor plan labels: PORCH 35'-8" x 7'-7", KITCHEN 16'-7" x 11'-9", BEDROOM 1 10'-0" x 15'-4", STORAGE, FAMILY 20'-0" x 13'-8", BEDROOM 2 12'-8" x 10'-0", COATS, PORCH 35'-8" x 7'-7")

© Copyright by
designer/architect

Plan #F12-013D-0133

Dimensions:	36' W x 42'4" D
Heated Sq. Ft.:	953
Bedrooms: 2	**Bathrooms:** 1½

Foundation: Crawl space standard; basement or slab for an additional fee

See index for more information

Images provided by
designer/architect

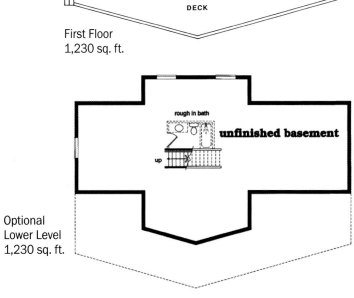

First Floor
1,230 sq. ft.

**Optional
Lower Level**
1,230 sq. ft.

rough in bath

unfinished basement

up

Plan #F12-062D-0047

Dimensions:	55'6" W x 30' D
Heated Sq. Ft.:	1,230
Bonus Sq. Ft.:	1,230
Bedrooms: 3	Bathrooms: 2
Exterior Walls:	2" x 6"

Foundation: Crawl space or basement, please specify when ordering

See index for more information

Images provided by designer/architect

br2 9'2x10'4
br3 9'2x10'4
mbr 13'2x11'4
liv 21'x15' VAULTED
din 10'x11'4
k 10' x 11'8
W S
DECK

© Copyright by designer/architect

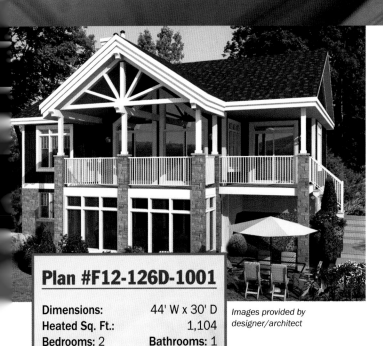

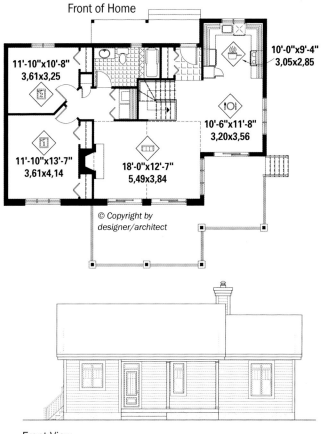

Front of Home

11'-10"x10'-8"
3,61x3,25

10'-0"x9'-4"
3,05x2,85

10'-6"x11'-8"
3,20x3,56

11'-10"x13'-7"
3,61x4,14

18'-0"x12'-7"
5,49x3,84

© Copyright by designer/architect

Front View

Plan #F12-126D-1001

Dimensions:	44' W x 30' D
Heated Sq. Ft.:	1,104
Bedrooms: 2	Bathrooms: 1
Exterior Walls:	2" x 6"
Foundation:	Basement

See index for more information

Images provided by designer/architect

Plan #F12-101D-0125

Dimensions:	118'3" W x 70' D
Heated Sq. Ft.:	2,970
Bonus Sq. Ft.:	2,014
Bedrooms: 2	Bathrooms: 2½
Exterior Walls:	2" x 6"
Foundation:	Walk-out basement

See index for more information

Features

- This rustic modern masterpiece offers an open concept floor plan with the utmost style and distinction
- Step into the foyer and be greeted by an open and expansive great room topped with a stunning ceiling
- The bright and stylish kitchen has a huge island, rustic beams above and plenty of cabinetspace for maintaining a sleek appearance free of clutter
- The first floor master bedroom enjoys a beamed ceiling, covered deck access, a luxury bath and a huge walk-in closet
- A guest room with its own private bath can be found on the opposite side of the first floor from the master bedroom for extra privacy
- The optional lower level has an additional 2,014 square feet of living area including a wet bar with island, a rec room, a game nook, three additional bedrooms, one full bath and a half bath
- 2-car front entry garage, and a 1-car side entry garage

Images provided by designer/architect

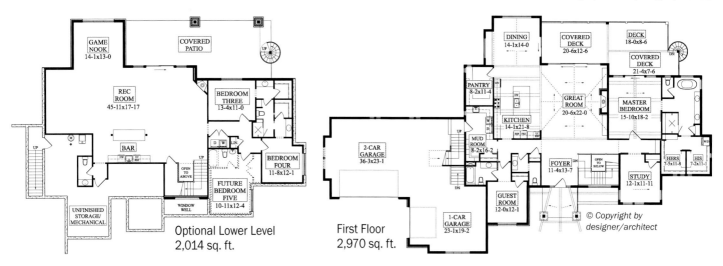

Optional Lower Level
2,014 sq. ft.

First Floor
2,970 sq. ft.

© Copyright by designer/architect

Plan #F12-056D-0098

Dimensions: 84'10" W x 61' D
Heated Sq. Ft.: 3,123
Bedrooms: 4   **Bathrooms:** 3
Foundation: Basement standard;
crawl space or slab for an
additional fee
See index for more information

Images provided by designer/architect

First Floor
1,876 sq. ft.

Lower Level
1,247 sq. ft.

© Copyright by
designer/architect

Features

- This home was just made for lake living right down to the "lake room" which shares a see-through fireplace with the screened porch allowing the homeowners to enjoy both a cozy fireplace indoors and outdoors
- The kitchen island is positioned so it easily takes in rear views
- The master bedroom enjoys a vaulted ceiling
- The lower level has a large social room, a shop area, two bedrooms, and a full bath
- 2-car front entry garage

Plan #F12-080D-0012

Dimensions:	36' W x 46'6" D
Heated Sq. Ft.:	1,370
Bedrooms: 3	**Bathrooms:** 2
Exterior Walls:	2" x 6"

Foundation: Crawl space or basement, please specify when ordering

See index for more information

Features

- The great room is open and bright and has an area with a two-story ceiling topped with skylights

- An enormous deck surrounds the rear of this home providing plenty of space for relaxing and dining in the great outdoors

- The second floor vaulted master bedroom has a private covered balcony and interesting interior windows that provide additional light and distinction

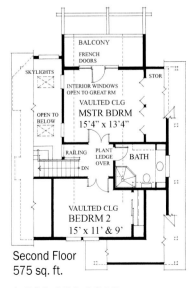

Images provided by designer/architect

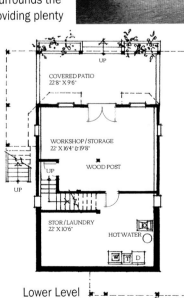

Lower Level

First Floor
795 sq. ft.

Second Floor
575 sq. ft.

Plan #F12-028D-0103

Dimensions:	40' W x 46' D
Heated Sq. Ft.:	1,520
Bedrooms: 2	**Bathrooms:** 1
Exterior Walls:	2" x 6"
Foundation:	Crawl space

See index for more information

Images provided by
designer/architect

BEDROOM 2
16' X 12'

CLO.
7'X8'

BEDROOM 1
17'X12'

CLO.
10'X3'

DINING
AREA
14' X 10'

BATH/LAUNDRY
17' X 10'

GREAT ROOM
22' X 16'

KITCHEN
18' X 12'

8' DEEP COVERED PORCH

© Copyright by
designer/architect

Plan #F12-013D-0218

Dimensions:	67'6" W x 22'8" D
Heated Sq. Ft.:	1,500
Bonus Sq. Ft.:	3,124
Bedrooms: 2	**Bathrooms:** 2½

Foundation: Walk-out basement
standard; crawl space or slab for
an additional fee

See index for more information

Images provided by
designer/architect

Optional
Second Floor
1,361 sq. ft.

BONUS / STORAGE
66'-10" x 24'-4"

© Copyright by
designer/architect

DECK
27'-2" x 9'-8"

SCREENED PORCH
27'-2" x 6'-6"

WORK AREA

MASTER
SUITE
16'-2" x 15'-4"

COUNTRY
KITCHEN
18'-2" x 15'-2"

3 CAR GARAGE
21'-6" x 37'-8"

GUEST
SUITE
14'-4" x 15'-2"

FAMILY
21'-8" x 15'-4"

First Floor
1,500 sq. ft.

PORCH
24'-3" x 7'-8"

BEDROOM 4
11'-4" x 13'-3"

BEDROOM 3
11'-4" x 13'-3"

LAUNDRY
7'-6" x 6'-4"

FAMILY
RECREATION
17'-3" x 22'-0"

HOME
OFFICE
11'-3" x 14'-6"

EXERCISE
AREA
11'-2" x 14'-10"

HOME
THEATER
27'-2" x 15'-0"

Optional Lower Level
1,763 sq. ft.

houseplansandmore.com

© Copyright by designer/architect

First Floor
1,064 sq. ft.

Second Floor
613 sq. ft.

Plan #F12-144D-0001

Images provided by designer/architect

Dimensions:	28' W x 40' D
Heated Sq. Ft.:	1,677
Bedrooms: 2	Bathrooms: 2
Exterior Walls:	2" x 6"

Foundation: Crawl space standard; slab for an additional fee

See index for more information

Plan #F12-101D-0147

Images provided by designer/architect

Dimensions:	87'6" W x 68' D
Heated Sq. Ft.:	2,538
Bonus Sq. Ft.:	1,276
Bedrooms: 1	Bathrooms: 2½
Exterior Walls:	2" x 6"

Foundation: Basement, daylight basement or walk-out basement, please specify when ordering

See index for more information

© Copyright by designer/architect

First Floor
2,538 sq. ft.

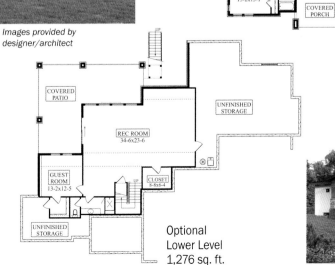

Optional Lower Level
1,276 sq. ft.

Plan #F12-123D-0263

Dimensions: 36' W x 23' D
Heated Sq. Ft.: 756
Bedrooms: 1   **Bathrooms:** 1
Foundation: Slab standard; crawl space, basement or walk-out basement for an additional fee

See index for more information

Features

- Little, but mighty this small getaway home is far from "roughing it" with its open-concept floor plan that makes it feel much larger than its true size
- Enter through a mud room entrance and find a small coat closet on the left and a built-in bench with hooks above on the right
- The kitchen is completely open to the great room and dining area for maximum function and an airy atmosphere
- The bedroom is directly across from the bathroom making it very convenient
- A stackable washer and dryer fits nicely into a centrally located closet

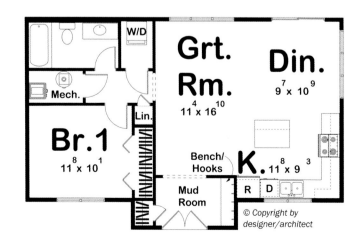

Images provided by designer/architect

© Copyright by designer/architect

Plan #F12-056D-0096

Dimensions:	91'6" W x 70' D
Heated Sq. Ft.:	2,510
Bonus Sq. Ft.:	2,510
Bedrooms: 3	**Bathrooms:** 2½

Foundation: Basement standard; crawl space or slab for an additional fee

See index for more information

Images provided by designer/architect

Features

- This wonderful home is designed in the popular Modern Farmhouse style

- A vaulted lodge room is connected to the kitchen and breakfast area and has covered porch views

- Both mud and laundry rooms make this home highly efficient

- The split bedroom floor plan has the master suite separated from the other bedrooms for privacy

- The optional lower level has an additional 2,510 square feet of living area with three additional bedrooms for guests, a wine cellar, a wet bar, a cards room, and a theater

- 2-car side entry garage

© Copyright by designer/architect

First Floor
2,510 sq. ft.

Optional Lower Level
2,510 sq. ft.

Plan #F12-101D-0115

Dimensions:	60' W x 76' D
Heated Sq. Ft.:	2,251
Bonus Sq. Ft.:	1,109
Bedrooms: 3	**Bathrooms:** 2½
Exterior Walls:	2" x 6"

Foundation: Basement or daylight basement, please specify when ordering

See index for more information

Images provided by designer/architect

Features

- This stylish rustic home has a great size for easy maintenance and a floor plan that offers privacy for all those who live there
- The great room with fireplace is open to the kitchen and dining area
- Study/bedroom #3 is a versatile space that can adapt to your needs
- A lovely covered deck extends off the great room3-car side entry
- The optional lower level has an additional 1,109 square feet of living area with a wet bar, recreation room, an additional bedroom, and a full bath
- 3-car front entry garage

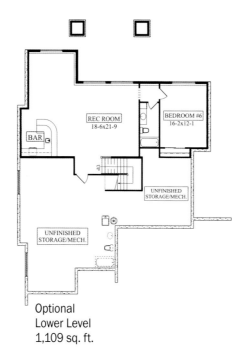

Optional
Lower Level
1,109 sq. ft.

First Floor
2,251 sq. ft.

Plan #F12-013D-0240

Dimensions:	57'10" W x 66'4" D
Heated Sq. Ft.:	2,799
Bonus Sq. Ft.:	2,454
Bedrooms: 4	Bathrooms: 4½
Exterior Walls:	2" x 6"

Foundation: Walk-out basement standard; crawl space or slab for an additional fee

See index for more information

Features

- This home offers plenty of room for growth and has a walk-out basement that makes it ideal for a sloping waterfront lot
- The kitchen has a huge built-in island with dining space and a walk-in pantry to keep everything organized
- The optional lower level has an additional 2,054 square feet of living area, while the second floor bonus room has an additional 400 square feet of living area
- 3-car side entry garage

Images provided by designer/architect

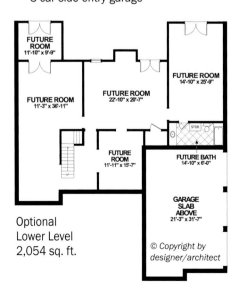

Optional
Lower Level
2,054 sq. ft.

© Copyright by
designer/architect

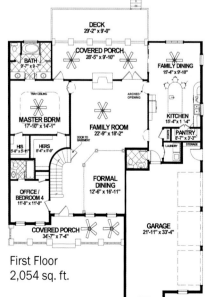

First Floor
2,054 sq. ft.

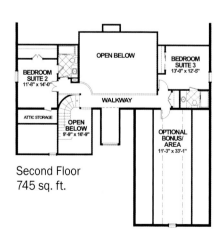

Second Floor
745 sq. ft.

Plan #F12-032D-0368

Dimensions:	36' W x 36' D
Heated Sq. Ft.:	1,625
Bedrooms: 3	Bathrooms: 2
Exterior Walls:	2" x 6"

Foundation: Basement standard; crawl space, floating slab or monolithic slab for an additional fee

See index for more information

Images provided by designer/architect

Features

- The great room features an awesome two-story tall vaulted ceiling
- A fireplace and a large balcony create an enchanting atmosphere in the great room
- Plenty of cabinets and counterspace are found throughout the spacious kitchen
- The first floor master bedroom enjoys a walk-in closet and a large bath nearby
- Two spacious bedrooms share a bath on the second floor, and are able to take in impressive views from the balcony overlooking the great room below

© Copyright by designer/architect

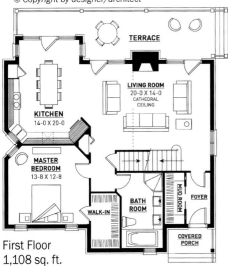

First Floor
1,108 sq. ft.

Second Floor
517 sq. ft.

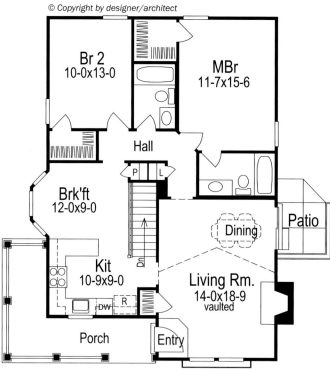

© Copyright by designer/architect

Images provided by designer/architect

Plan #F12-007D-0105

Dimensions: 35' W x 40'8" D
Heated Sq. Ft.: 1,084
Bedrooms: 2   **Bathrooms:** 2
Foundation: Basement standard; crawl space or slab for an additional fee

See index for more information

Br 2
10-0x13-0

MBr
11-7x15-6

Hall

P   L

Brk'ft
12-0x9-0

Dining

Patio

Kit
10-9x9-0

Living Rm.
14-0x18-9
vaulted

DW   R

Porch

Entry

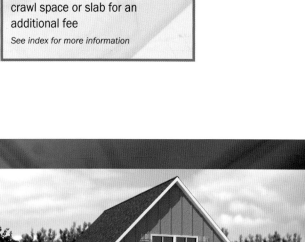

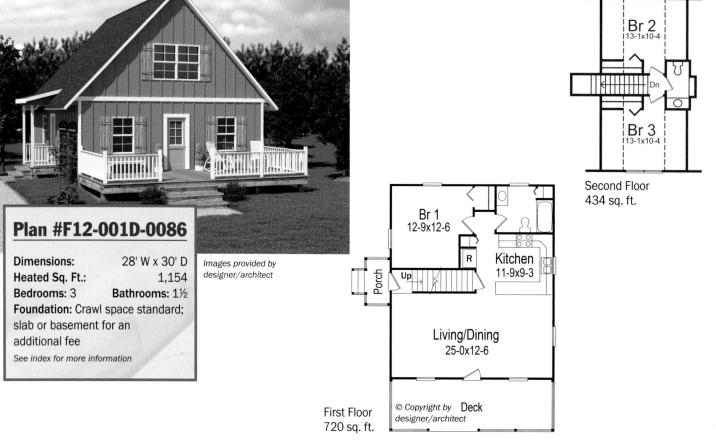

Plan #F12-001D-0086

Dimensions: 28' W x 30' D
Heated Sq. Ft.: 1,154
Bedrooms: 3   **Bathrooms:** 1½
Foundation: Crawl space standard; slab or basement for an additional fee

See index for more information

Images provided by designer/architect

Br 2
13-1x10-4

Br 3
13-1x10-4

Second Floor
434 sq. ft.

Br 1
12-9x12-6

Kitchen
11-9x9-3

R

Porch

Up

Living/Dining
25-0x12-6

First Floor
720 sq. ft.

© Copyright by designer/architect

Deck

Plan #F12-121D-0025

Dimensions: 50' W x 34'6" D
Heated Sq. Ft.: 1,368
Bedrooms: 3   **Bathrooms:** 2
Foundation: Basement standard; crawl space or slab for an additional fee

See index for more information

Images provided by designer/architect

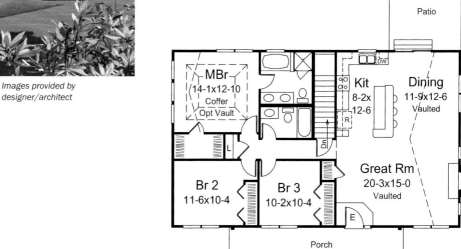

Garage
23-4x23-4

© Copyright by designer/architect

Patio

MBr
14-1x12-10
Coffer
Opt Vault

Kit
8-2x
12-6

Dining
11-9x12-6
Vaulted

DW

R

L

Dn

Br 2
11-6x10-4

Br 3
10-2x10-4

Great Rm
20-3x15-0
Vaulted

E

Porch

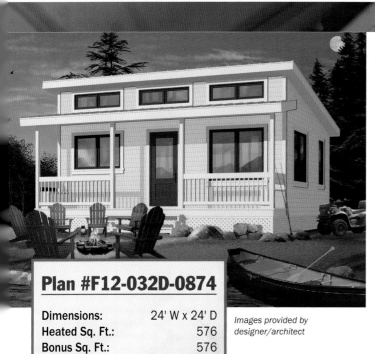

Plan #F12-032D-0874

Dimensions: 24' W x 24' D
Heated Sq. Ft.: 576
Bonus Sq. Ft.: 576
Bedrooms: 1   **Bathrooms:** 1
Exterior Walls: 2" x 6"
Foundation: Basement standard; crawl space, floating slab or monolithic slab for an additional fee

See index for more information

Images provided by designer/architect

First Floor
576 sq. ft.

12' - 4" x 9' - 1"

22' - 8" x 10' - 0"

24' - 0" x 6' - 0"

© Copyright by designer/architect

Optional Lower Level
576 sq. ft.

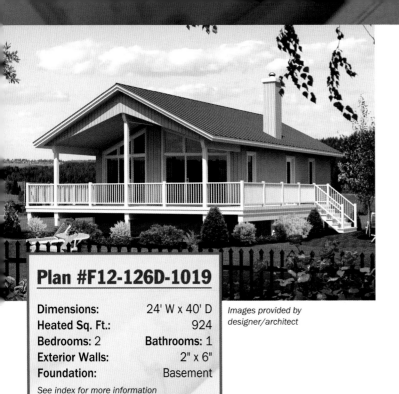

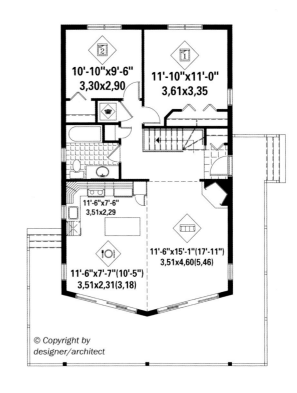

Plan #F12-126D-1019

Dimensions:	24' W x 40' D
Heated Sq. Ft.:	924
Bedrooms: 2	Bathrooms: 1
Exterior Walls:	2" x 6"
Foundation:	Basement

See index for more information

Images provided by designer/architect

10'-10"x9'-6"
3,30x2,90

11'-10"x11'-0"
3,61x3,35

11'-6"x7'-6"
3,51x2,29

11'-6"x15'-1"(17'-11")
3,51x4,60(5,46)

11'-6"x7'-7"(10'-5")
3,51x2,31(3,18)

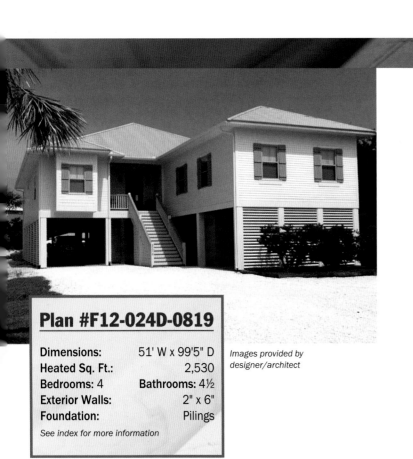

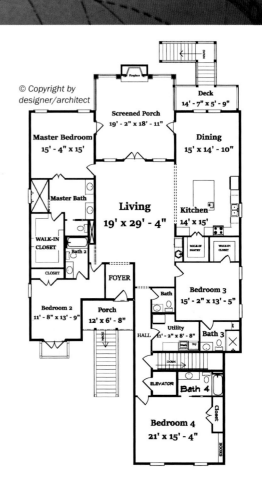

Plan #F12-024D-0819

Dimensions:	51' W x 99'5" D
Heated Sq. Ft.:	2,530
Bedrooms: 4	Bathrooms: 4½
Exterior Walls:	2" x 6"
Foundation:	Pilings

See index for more information

Images provided by designer/architect

Deck
14' - 7" x 5' - 9"

Screened Porch
19' - 2" x 18' - 11"

Master Bedroom
15' - 4" x 15'

Dining
15' x 14' - 10"

Master Bath

Living
19' x 29' - 4"

Kitchen
14' x 15'

WALK-IN CLOSET

Bath 2

CLOSET

FOYER

Bedroom 3
15' - 2" x 13' - 5"

Bedroom 2
11' - 8" x 13' - 9"

Porch
12' x 6' - 8"

Bath

Utility
11' - 2" x 8' - 8"

HALL

Bath 3

ELEVATOR

Bath 4

Bedroom 4
21' 15' - 4"

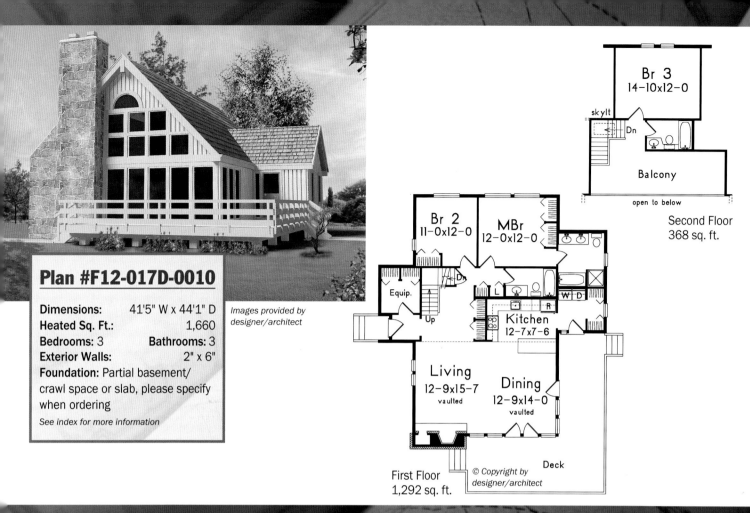

Plan #F12-017D-0010

Dimensions:	41'5" W x 44'1" D
Heated Sq. Ft.:	1,660
Bedrooms: 3	Bathrooms: 3
Exterior Walls:	2" x 6"

Foundation: Partial basement/
crawl space or slab, please specify
when ordering

See index for more information

*Images provided by
designer/architect*

Br 3
14-10x12-0

skylt

Dn

Balcony

open to below

Second Floor
368 sq. ft.

Br 2
11-0x12-0

MBr
12-0x12-0

Equip.

Up

Kitchen
12-7x7-6

Living
12-9x15-7
vaulted

Dining
12-9x14-0
vaulted

Deck

© Copyright by
designer/architect

First Floor
1,292 sq. ft.

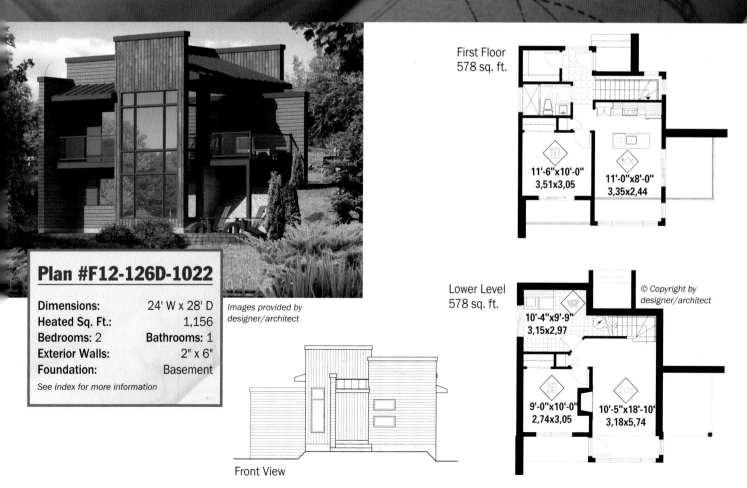

Plan #F12-126D-1022

Dimensions:	24' W x 28' D
Heated Sq. Ft.:	1,156
Bedrooms: 2	Bathrooms: 1
Exterior Walls:	2" x 6"
Foundation:	Basement

See index for more information

*Images provided by
designer/architect*

First Floor
578 sq. ft.

11'-6"x10'-0"
3,51x3,05

11'-0"x8'-0"
3,35x2,44

Lower Level
578 sq. ft.

© Copyright by
designer/architect

10'-4"x9'-9"
3,15x2,97

9'-0"x10'-0"
2,74x3,05

10'-5"x18'-10'
3,18x5,74

Front View

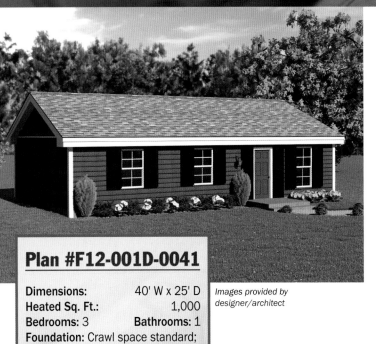

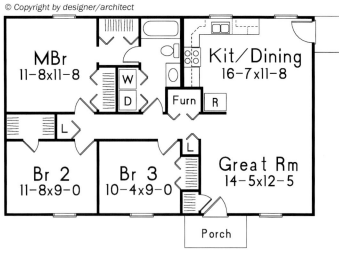

© Copyright by designer/architect

MBr
11-8x11-8

Kit/Dining
16-7x11-8

W
D
Furn
R

L

Br 2
11-8x9-0

Br 3
10-4x9-0

L

Great Rm
14-5x12-5

Porch

Plan #F12-001D-0041

Dimensions:	40' W x 25' D
Heated Sq. Ft.:	1,000
Bedrooms: 3	**Bathrooms:** 1

Foundation: Crawl space standard; basement or slab for an additional fee

See index for more information

Images provided by designer/architect

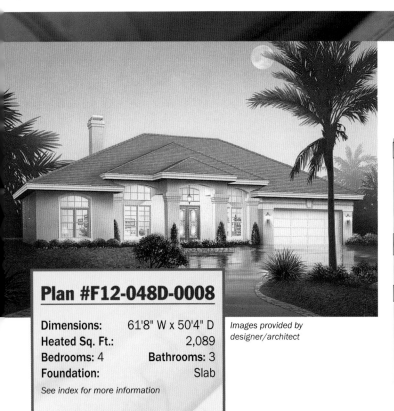

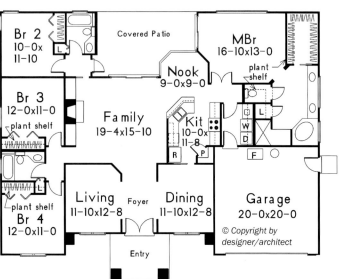

Br 2
10-0x
11-10

L

Covered Patio

MBr
16-10x13-0

plant shelf

Nook
9-0x9-0

Br 3
12-0x11-0

plant shelf

Family
19-4x15-10

Kit
10-0x
11-8

W
D
L

R
P
F

Living
11-10x12-8

Foyer

Dining
11-10x12-8

Garage
20-0x20-0

plant shelf

Br 4
12-0x11-0

Entry

© Copyright by designer/architect

Plan #F12-048D-0008

Dimensions:	61'8" W x 50'4" D
Heated Sq. Ft.:	2,089
Bedrooms: 4	**Bathrooms:** 3
Foundation:	Slab

See index for more information

Images provided by designer/architect

Front of Home

FRONT PORCH

© Copyright by designer/architect

BEDROOM 1
10-0 X 11-2

BATH ROOM

FOYER

BEDROOM 2
10-2 X 8-0

FAMILY ROOM
18-6 X 11-2

KITCHEN
16-2 X 11-2

TERRACE

Images provided by designer/architect

Front View

Plan #F12-032D-0357

Dimensions: 36' W x 24' D
Heated Sq. Ft.: 874
Bedrooms: 2   **Bathrooms:** 1
Exterior Walls: 2" x 6"
Foundation: Crawl space standard; monolithic slab or floating slab for an additional fee

See index for more information

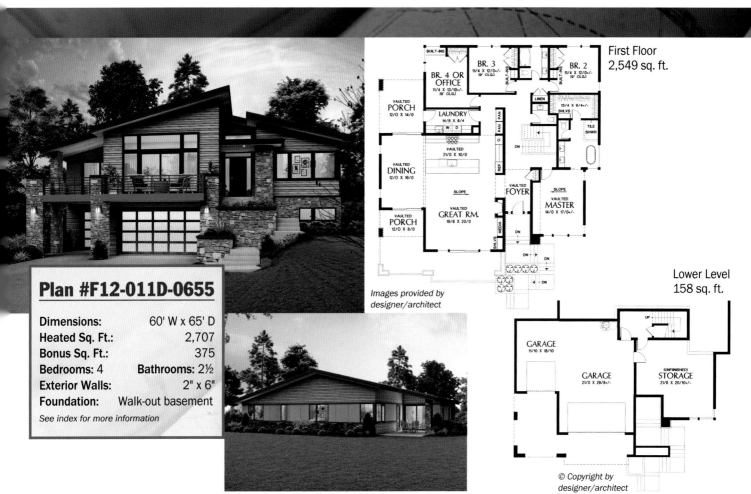

First Floor
2,549 sq. ft.

BUILT-INS

BR. 4 OR OFFICE
11/4 X 13/10+/-
(9' CLG.)

BR. 3
11/4 X 12/0+/-
(9' CLG.)

BR. 2
11/4 X 12/0+/-
(9' CLG.)

VAULTED **PORCH**
12/0 X 14/0

LAUNDRY
14/8 X 8/4

LINEN

SHLVS.

11/4 X 6/4+/-

TILE SHWR.

VAULTED **DINING**
12/0 X 19/0

21/0 X 10/0

DN

VAULTED **MASTER**
14/0 X 17/0+/-

VAULTED **PORCH**
12/0 X 8/0

SLOPE

VAULTED **GREAT RM.**
19/8 X 20/0

VAULTED **FOYER**

SLOPE

MEDIA

DN

DN

DN

DN

Images provided by designer/architect

Lower Level
158 sq. ft.

UP

GARAGE
11/10 X 18/10

GARAGE
21/0 X 29/8+/-

(UNFINISHED) STORAGE
21/6 X 20/10+/-

© Copyright by designer/architect

Plan #F12-011D-0655

Dimensions: 60' W x 65' D
Heated Sq. Ft.: 2,707
Bonus Sq. Ft.: 375
Bedrooms: 4   **Bathrooms:** 2½
Exterior Walls: 2" x 6"
Foundation: Walk-out basement

See index for more information

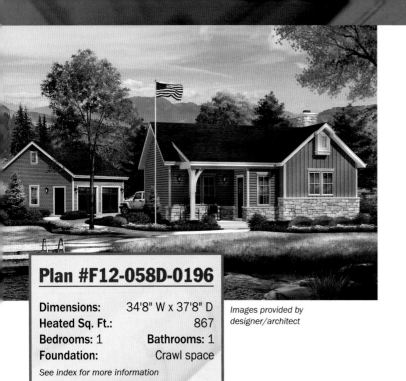

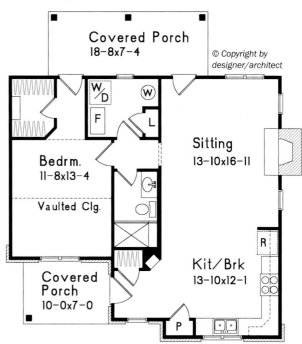

Covered Porch 18-8x7-4

© Copyright by designer/architect

W/D
F
W
L

Bedrm. 11-8x13-4

Vaulted Clg.

Sitting 13-10x16-11

R

Kit/Brk 13-10x12-1

Covered Porch 10-0x7-0

P

Plan #F12-058D-0196

Dimensions:	34'8" W x 37'8" D
Heated Sq. Ft.:	867
Bedrooms: 1	**Bathrooms:** 1
Foundation:	Crawl space

See index for more information

Images provided by designer/architect

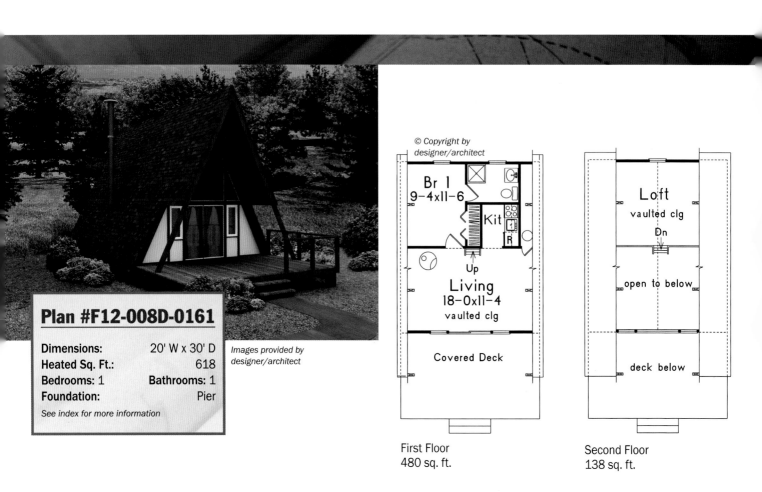

Plan #F12-008D-0161

Dimensions:	20' W x 30' D
Heated Sq. Ft.:	618
Bedrooms: 1	**Bathrooms:** 1
Foundation:	Pier

See index for more information

Images provided by designer/architect

© Copyright by designer/architect

Br 1 9-4x11-6

Kit

R

Up

Living 18-0x11-4 vaulted clg

Covered Deck

Loft vaulted clg

Dn

open to below

deck below

First Floor 480 sq. ft.

Second Floor 138 sq. ft.

Plan #F12-058D-0199

Dimensions:	32'4" W x 48' D
Heated Sq. Ft.:	1,158
Bedrooms: 2	**Bathrooms:** 2
Foundation:	Crawl space

See index for more information

Images provided by designer/architect

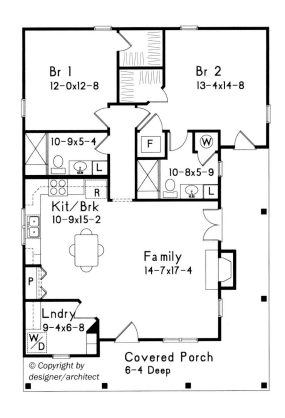

Br 1
12-0x12-8

Br 2
13-4x14-8

10-9x5-4

F

W

10-8x5-9

R

Kit/Brk
10-9x15-2

Family
14-7x17-4

P

Lndry
9-4x6-8

W/D

Covered Porch
6-4 Deep

© Copyright by designer/architect

Plan #F12-141D-0442

Dimensions:	44' W x 44' D
Heated Sq. Ft.:	1,727
Bonus Sq. Ft.:	300
Bedrooms: 2	**Bathrooms:** 2
Exterior Walls:	2" x 6"
Foundation: Slab standard; crawl space for an additional fee	

See index for more information

Images provided by designer/architect

CLOSET
11 x 10

SHWR
5 x 4

BATH
6 x 5

KITCHEN
17 x 11

PORCH BELOW

UTILITY
11 x 4

HALL

BEDROOM #1
14 x 19

'VAULTED' FAMILY ROOM
22 x 19

Second Floor
1,292 sq. ft.

'VAULTED' COVERED BALCONY
30 x 10

BEDROOM #2
13 x 11

BATH #2
7 x 7

ENTRY

PORCH
12 x 6

© Copyright by designer/architect

STORAGE
15 x 22

DOUBLE GARAGE
22 x 22

9' X 9' GARAGE DOOR

9' X 9' GARAGE DOOR

STOOP

BALCONY ABOVE

First Floor
435 sq. ft.

300 S.F.
ART LOFT
15 x 19

Optional Third Floor
300 sq. ft.

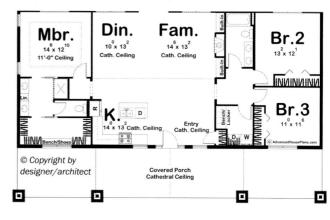

© Copyright by
designer/architect

Mbr.
14 x 12⁶
11'-0" Ceiling

Din.
10 x 13²

Fam.
14 x 13²
Cath. Ceiling

Br.2
13 x 12¹

K.
14 x 13² Cath. Ceiling

Entry
Cath. Ceiling

Br.3
11 x 11⁰

Bench/Shoes

Covered Porch
Cathedral Ceiling

© AdvancedHousePlans.com

Images provided by
designer/architect

Plan #F12-123D-0258

Dimensions:	62' W x 38' D
Heated Sq. Ft.:	1,695
Bedrooms: 3	**Bathrooms:** 2
Exterior Walls:	2" x 6"

Foundation: Slab standard; crawl space, basement or walk-out basement for an additional fee

See index for more information

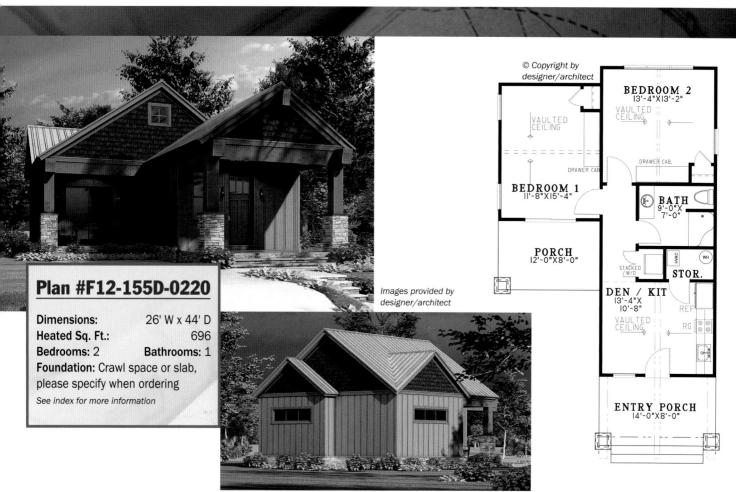

Plan #F12-155D-0220

Dimensions:	26' W x 44' D
Heated Sq. Ft.:	696
Bedrooms: 2	**Bathrooms:** 1

Foundation: Crawl space or slab, please specify when ordering

See index for more information

© Copyright by
designer/architect

BEDROOM 2
13'-4"X13'-2"
VAULTED
CEILING

VAULTED
CEILING

DRAWER CAB.

DRAWER CAB.

BEDROOM 1
11'-8"X15'-4"

BATH
9'-0"X
7'-0"

PORCH
12'-0"X8'-0"

STACKED
W/D

HVAC

WH

STOR.

DEN / KIT
13'-4"X
10'-8"
VAULTED
CEILING

REF

RG

Images provided by
designer/architect

ENTRY PORCH
14'-0"X8'-0"

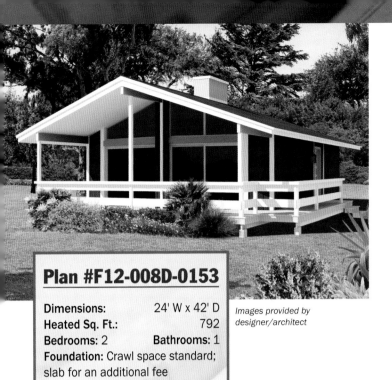

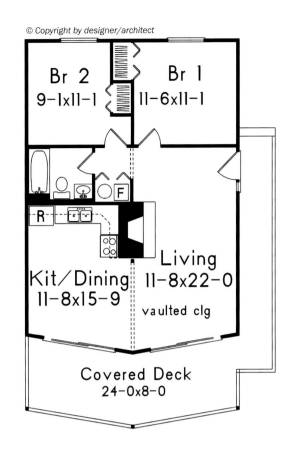

© Copyright by designer/architect

Br 2
9-1x11-1

Br 1
11-6x11-1

R

Kit/Dining
11-8x15-9

Living
11-8x22-0
vaulted clg

Covered Deck
24-0x8-0

Plan #F12-008D-0153

Images provided by designer/architect

Dimensions:	24' W x 42' D
Heated Sq. Ft.:	792
Bedrooms: 2	**Bathrooms:** 1

Foundation: Crawl space standard; slab for an additional fee

See index for more information

Br 3
11-0x12-0

Study
10-8x12-0

Patio

Garage
22-10x20-1

© Copyright by designer/architect

Great Room
20-1x19-5
vaulted clg

Br 2
11-0x10-0

plant shelf above

Laun.

Kit/Dining
20-0x19-0

Entry

MBr
17-4x14-0
vaulted clg

Porch

Porch

Plan #F12-007D-0055

Images provided by designer/architect

Dimensions:	67' W x 51'4" D
Heated Sq. Ft.:	2,029
Bedrooms: 3	**Bathrooms:** 2

Foundation: Basement standard; crawl space or slab for an additional fee

See index for more information

call toll-free 1-800-373-2646

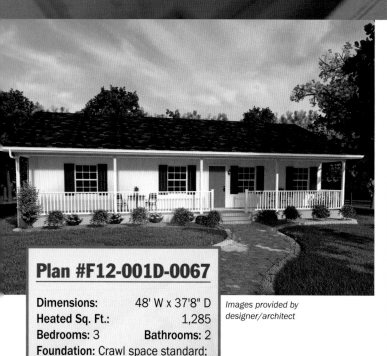

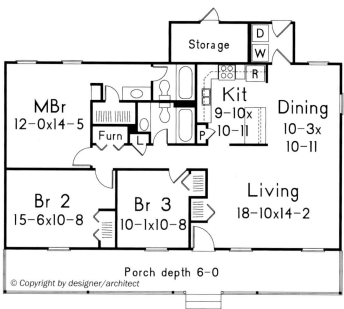

Plan #F12-001D-0067

Dimensions: 48' W x 37'8" D
Heated Sq. Ft.: 1,285
Bedrooms: 3   Bathrooms: 2
Foundation: Crawl space standard; basement or slab for an additional fee

See index for more information

Images provided by designer/architect

Storage

D
W

MBr
12-0x14-5

Furn

Kit
9-10x
10-11

R
P

Dining
10-3x
10-11

Br 2
15-6x10-8

Br 3
10-1x10-8

Living
18-10x14-2

Porch depth 6-0

© Copyright by designer/architect

Plan #F12-011D-0637

Dimensions: 46'6" W x 54' D
Heated Sq. Ft.: 1,744
Bedrooms: 3   Bathrooms: 2½
Exterior Walls: 2" x 6"
Foundation: Crawl space or slab standard; basement for an additional fee

See index for more information

Images provided by designer/architect

VAULTED
DINING
10/6 X 12/8

6/4 X 7/10

MASTER
12/4 X 16/10
(9' CLG.)

VAULTED
GREAT RM.
16/6 X 21/6

(9' CLG.)

BUILT-INS

VAULTED
10/0 X 14/10

W D

6/4 X 8/4

TILE
SHWR

(9' CLG.)

PAN

LIN LIN

BKS

REF

GARAGE
19/0 X 22/0

VAULTED
BR. 3
10/0 X 11/4

VAULTED
BR. 2
10/0 X 13/0

© Copyright by designer/architect

First Floor
2,104 sq. ft.

Optional
Second Floor
268 sq. ft.

Images provided by
designer/architect

Plan #F12-011D-0617

Dimensions: 69' W x 58' D
Heated Sq. Ft.: 2,104
Bonus Sq. Ft.: 268
Bedrooms: 3 **Bathrooms:** 2½
Exterior Walls: 2" x 6"
Foundation: Crawl space or slab
standard; basement for an
additional fee

See index for more information

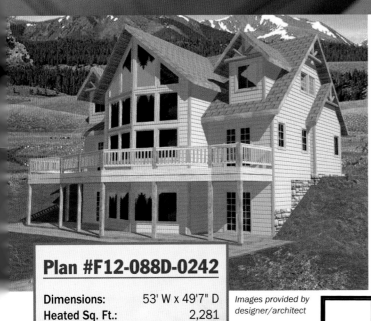

Plan #F12-088D-0242

Dimensions: 53' W x 49'7" D
Heated Sq. Ft.: 2,281
Bonus Sq. Ft.: 1,436
Bedrooms: 3 **Bathrooms:** 2½
Exterior Walls: 2" x 6"
Foundation: Walk-out basement

See index for more information

Images provided by
designer/architect

Second Floor
845 sq. ft.

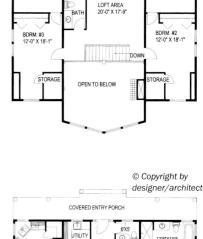

Optional
Lower Level
1,436 sq. ft.

First Floor
1,436 sq. ft.

Plan #F12-082S-0001

Dimensions: 121'4" W x 78'4" D
Heated Sq. Ft.:   6,816
Bedrooms: 4   **Bathrooms:** 7½
Foundation: Basement or walk-out basement, please specify when ordering

See index for more information

Features

- The first floor features an abundance of amenities including a two-story great room with fireplace and an enchanting sun porch
- Three additional bedroom suites and a studio for guests are offered on the second floor
- The lower level includes an amazing media room, computer/game room, office and a second kitchen
- 2-car front entry garage, 2-car side entry carport

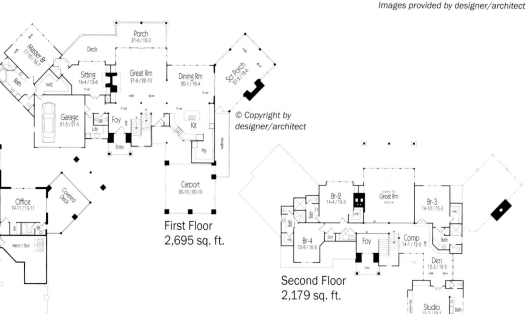

Images provided by designer/architect

© Copyright by designer/architect

First Floor
2,695 sq. ft.

Lower Level
1,942 sq. ft.

Second Floor
2,179 sq. ft.

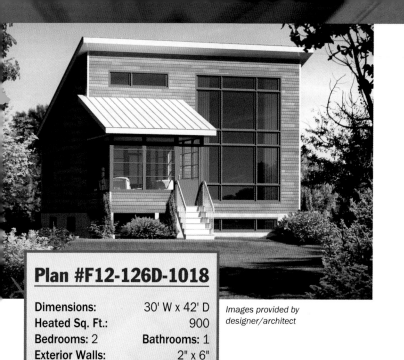

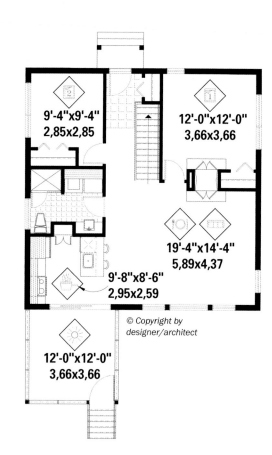

Plan #F12-126D-1018

Dimensions:	30' W x 42' D
Heated Sq. Ft.:	900
Bedrooms: 2	Bathrooms: 1
Exterior Walls:	2" x 6"
Foundation:	Basement

See index for more information

Images provided by designer/architect

9'-4"x9'-4"
2,85x2,85

12'-0"x12'-0"
3,66x3,66

19'-4"x14'-4"
5,89x4,37

9'-8"x8'-6"
2,95x2,59

12'-0"x12'-0"
3,66x3,66

© Copyright by designer/architect

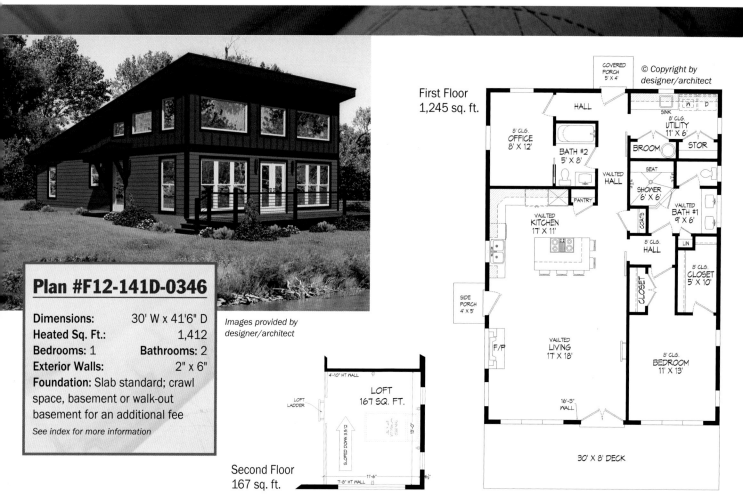

Plan #F12-141D-0346

Dimensions:	30' W x 41'6" D
Heated Sq. Ft.:	1,412
Bedrooms: 1	Bathrooms: 2
Exterior Walls:	2" x 6"
Foundation:	Slab standard; crawl space, basement or walk-out basement for an additional fee

See index for more information

Images provided by designer/architect

First Floor
1,245 sq. ft.

Second Floor
167 sq. ft.

Plan #F12-011D-0679

Dimensions:	53' W x 58' D
Heated Sq. Ft.:	1,821
Bedrooms: 3	Bathrooms: 2
Exterior Walls:	2" x 6"

Foundation: Crawl space or slab standard; basement for an additional fee

See index for more information

Images provided by designer/architect

© Copyright by designer/architect

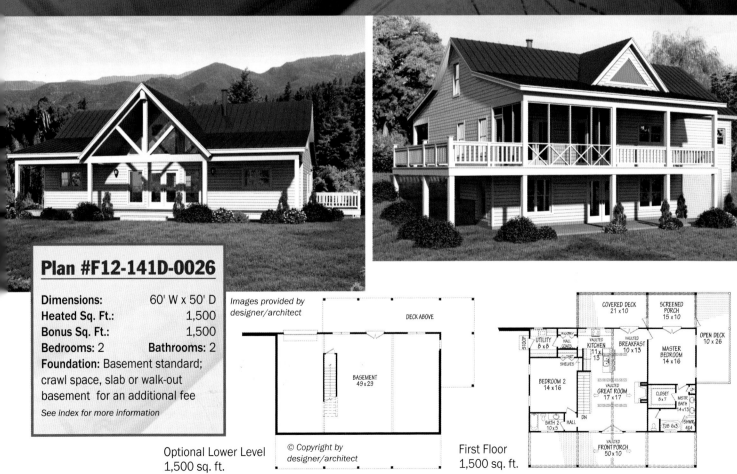

Plan #F12-141D-0026

Dimensions:	60' W x 50' D
Heated Sq. Ft.:	1,500
Bonus Sq. Ft.:	1,500
Bedrooms: 2	Bathrooms: 2

Foundation: Basement standard; crawl space, slab or walk-out basement for an additional fee

See index for more information

Images provided by designer/architect

Optional Lower Level
1,500 sq. ft.

© Copyright by designer/architect

First Floor
1,500 sq. ft.

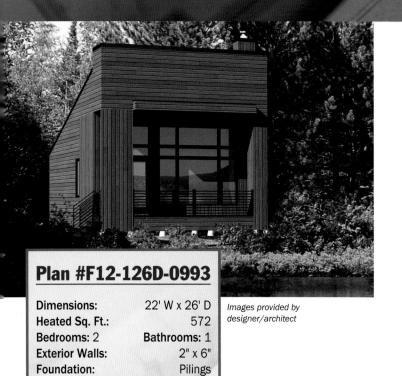

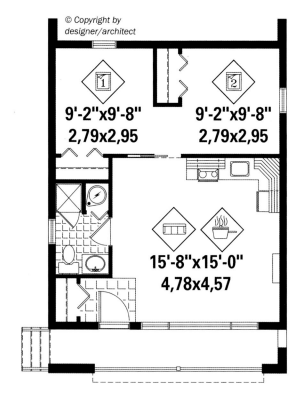

Plan #F12-126D-0993

Dimensions:	22' W x 26' D
Heated Sq. Ft.:	572
Bedrooms: 2	Bathrooms: 1
Exterior Walls:	2" x 6"
Foundation:	Pilings

See index for more information

Images provided by designer/architect

© Copyright by designer/architect

9'-2"x9'-8"
2,79x2,95

9'-2"x9'-8"
2,79x2,95

15'-8"x15'-0"
4,78x4,57

Plan #F12-144D-0017

Dimensions:	42' W x 34'6" D
Heated Sq. Ft.:	1,043
Bedrooms: 2	Bathrooms: 1
Exterior Walls:	2" x 6"
Foundation: Crawl space or slab, please specify when ordering	

See index for more information

Images provided by designer/architect

36" FR   DW
KITCHEN
16'5 X 10'0
EATING ISLAND 9'6" X 42"

H/W   W/D
MUD
5'5 X 9'5

(FAUX CEILING BEAMS ABOVE)
GAS FP.
VAULTED CEILING
LIVING RM.
16'5 X 14'11

41" HALL
41" HALL
6 FT CLOSET
OFFICE / GUEST
10'9 X 10'0

16" BENCH
SHOWER
42" X 66"
BATH
6'8 X 10'11

DRESSER   HI-BOY
W.I.C.
4'0 X 4'6

VAULTED CEILING
COVERED PATIO
22'6 X 12

M. BEDROOM
12'6 X 13'0
KING

8 FT CLOSET

© Copyright by designer/architect

Plan #F12-013D-0216

Dimensions:	42' W x 42' D
Heated Sq. Ft.:	1,488
Bedrooms: 2	Bathrooms: 2
Exterior Walls:	2" x 6"

Foundation: Crawl space standard; slab or basement for an additional fee

See index for more information

Images provided by designer/architect

© Copyright by designer/architect

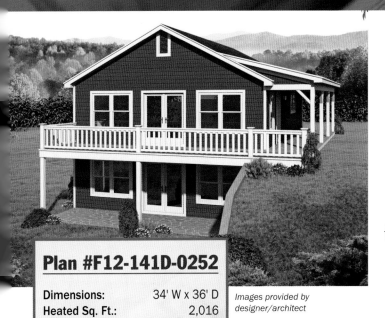

Plan #F12-141D-0252

Dimensions:	34' W x 36' D
Heated Sq. Ft.:	2,016
Bedrooms: 2	Bathrooms: 2
Exterior Walls:	2" x 6"

Foundation: Walk-out basement standard; crawl space, slab or basement for an additional fee

See index for more information

Images provided by designer/architect

Front View

Lower Level
1,008 sq. ft.

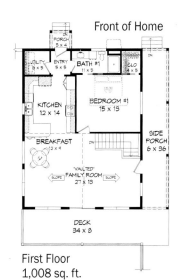

First Floor
1,008 sq. ft.

call toll-free 1-800-373-2646

Plan #F12-032D-1134

Dimensions:	40' W x 34'4" D
Heated Sq. Ft.:	2,652
Bedrooms: 4	**Bathrooms:** 2
Exterior Walls:	2" x 6"
Foundation:	Basement

See index for more information

Features

- This stylish Craftsman home has Modern Farmhouse flair thanks to its black window panes, white vertical siding and light fixture choices
- Right off the foyer is a handy enclosed mud room for keeping the rest of the house tidy
- The living and dining rooms are open to one another and are topped with a cathedral ceiling
- The kitchen features a huge corner walk-in pantry, an oversized island with seating and is open to the dining room
- The lower level has a spacious recreation area, two additional bedrooms, a full bath and the laundry room

Lower Level
1,326 sq. ft.

© Copyright by
designer/architect

First Floor
1,326 sq. ft.

Images provided by designer/architect

Plan #F12-011D-0627

Dimensions:	52' W x 61' D
Heated Sq. Ft.:	1,878
Bedrooms: 3	**Bathrooms:** 2
Exterior Walls:	2" x 6"

Foundation: Crawl space or slab standard; basement for an additional fee

See index for more information

Features

- Upon entering the foyer that is flanked by benches, there is a soaring 16' ceiling allowing for plenty of natural light to enter the space
- Beautiful family-friendly design with a centrally located great room, dining room and kitchen combination and the sleeping quarters in a private wing
- The master suite is complete with the amenities of a walk-in closet, a double-bowl vanity and separate tub and shower units in the private bath
- Enjoy outdoor living on the covered rear patio that has a built-in barbecue grill and cabinets for ease when cooking outdoors
- 2-car front entry garage

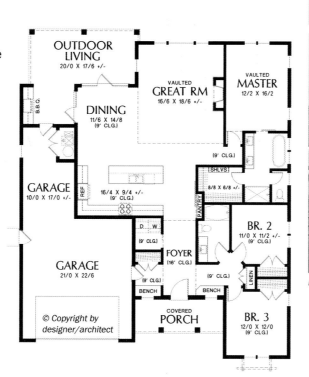

Images provided by designer/architect

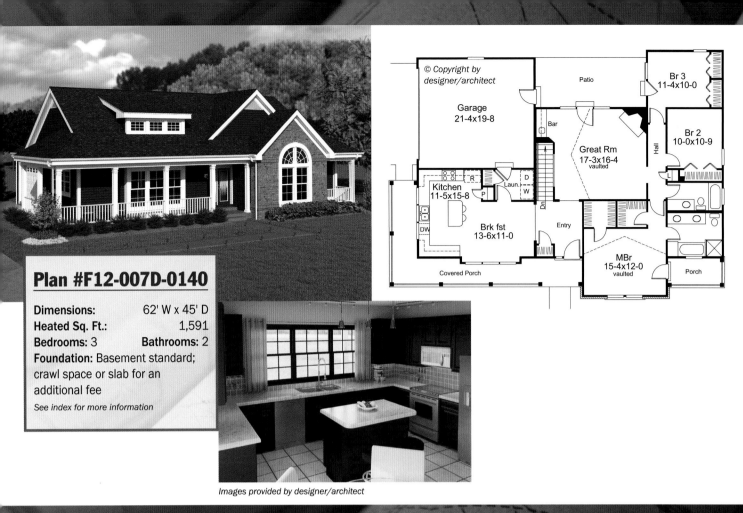

Plan #F12-007D-0140

Dimensions:	62' W x 45' D
Heated Sq. Ft.:	1,591
Bedrooms: 3	**Bathrooms:** 2

Foundation: Basement standard; crawl space or slab for an additional fee

See index for more information

Images provided by designer/architect

© Copyright by designer/architect

Garage 21-4x19-8

Patio

Br 3 11-4x10-0

Bar

Br 2 10-0x10-9

Great Rm 17-3x16-4 vaulted

Hall

Kitchen 11-5x15-8

Laun.

Entry

Brk fst 13-6x11-0

Covered Porch

MBr 15-4x12-0 vaulted

Porch

Plan #F12-032D-0935

Images provided by designer/architect

Dimensions:	24' W x 24' D
Heated Sq. Ft.:	1,050
Bedrooms: 2	**Bathrooms:** 1½
Exterior Walls:	2" x 6"

Foundation: Basement standard; crawl space, floating slab or monolithic slab for an additional fee

See index for more information

© Copyright by designer/architect

10'-2" X 9'-0" 3,05 X 2,70

12'-0" X 11'-0" 3,60 X 3,30

Second Floor 474 sq. ft.

11'-8" X 10'-4" 3,50 X 3,10

22'-8" X 12'-4" 6,80 X 3,70

First Floor 576 sq. ft.

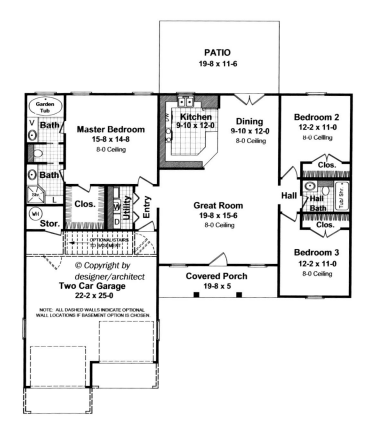

PATIO
19-8 x 11-6

Garden Tub

Bath
V

Bath

Shr.

L

WH

Stor.

Master Bedroom
15-8 x 14-8
8-0 Ceiling

Clos.

W
D

Utility

Entry

Kitchen
9-10 x 12-0

Dining
9-10 x 12-0
8-0 Ceiling

Great Room
19-8 x 15-6
8-0 Ceiling

Bedroom 2
12-2 x 11-0
8-0 Ceiling

Clos.

Hall

Tub/Shr.

Hall Bath

Clos.

Bedroom 3
12-2 x 11-0
8-0 Ceiling

OPTIONAL STAIRS TO BASEMENT

© Copyright by
designer/architect
Two Car Garage
22-2 x 25-0

Covered Porch
19-8 x 5

NOTE: ALL DASHED WALLS INDICATE OPTIONAL
WALL LOCATIONS IF BASEMENT OPTION IS CHOSEN.

Plan #F12-077D-0019

Images provided by designer/architect

Dimensions: 54' W x 47' D
Heated Sq. Ft.: 1,400
Bedrooms: 3   Bathrooms: 2
Foundation: Slab, crawl space, basement or walk-out basement, please specify when ordering

See index for more information

Plan #F12-111D-0074

Images provided by designer/architect

Dimensions: 39' W x 48'2" D
Heated Sq. Ft.: 2,005
Bedrooms: 3   Bathrooms: 3
Foundation: Slab standard; crawl space for an additional fee

See index for more information

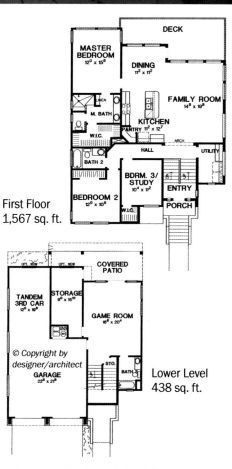

DECK

MASTER BEDROOM
12⁰ x 15⁸

DINING
11² x 11²

FAMILY ROOM
14⁸ x 19⁸

KITCHEN

M. BATH

W.I.C.

PANTRY 11² x 12⁷

HALL

UTILITY

ARCH.

BATH 2

BDRM. 3/
STUDY
10⁴ x 11²

ENTRY

BEDROOM 2
12⁰ x 10⁶

W.I.C.

PORCH

First Floor
1,567 sq. ft.

COVERED PATIO

TANDEM
3RD CAR
12⁰ x 19⁸

STORAGE
9⁰ x 15¹⁰

GAME ROOM
16⁸ x 20⁴

© Copyright by
designer/architect

GARAGE
22⁰ x 21⁸

STO.

BATH 3

Lower Level
438 sq. ft.

Plan #F12-101D-0057

Dimensions:	58' W x 90' D
Heated Sq. Ft.:	2,037
Bonus Sq. Ft.:	1,330
Bedrooms: 1	Bathrooms: 1½
Exterior Walls:	2" x 6"
Foundation:	Walk-out basement

See index for more information

Images provided by designer/architect

Features

- Enjoy the outdoors on both levels of this home with first floor and lower level covered patios and decks
- The front porch opens to an entry with a formal dining room and a staircase to the lower level
- The large U-shaped kitchen features space for casual dining as well as a wet bar for entertaining
- The master bedroom is in a wing to itself and features a stepped ceiling, a luxurious bath, and a large walk-in closet
- The optional lower level has an additional 1,330 square feet of living area and offers two additional bedrooms with full baths, an office, an open recreation area, a safe room, and unfinished storage
- 3-car side entry garage

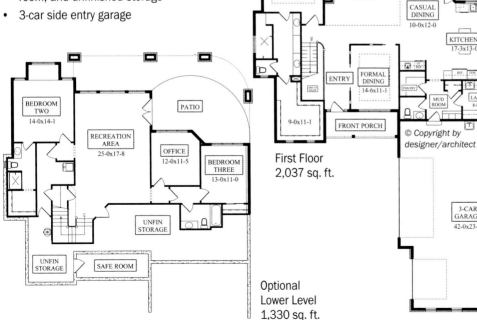

First Floor
2,037 sq. ft.

© Copyright by designer/architect

Optional
Lower Level
1,330 sq. ft.

houseplansandmore.com

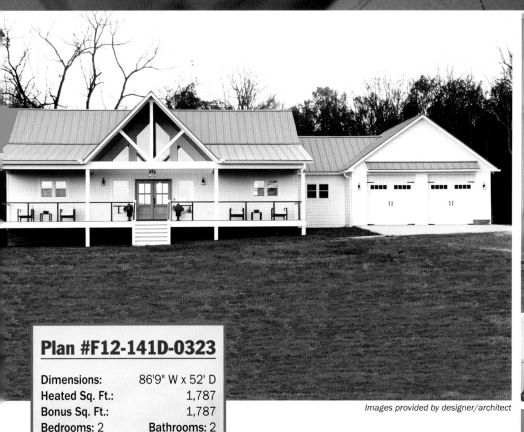

Images provided by designer/architect

Plan #F12-141D-0323

Dimensions:	86'9" W x 52' D
Heated Sq. Ft.:	1,787
Bonus Sq. Ft.:	1,787
Bedrooms: 2	**Bathrooms:** 2

Foundation: Slab standard; crawl space, basement or walk-out basement for an additional fee

See index for more information

Features

- Perfect symmetry embodies this truly special Modern Farmhouse design
- From the large covered front porch, step right into the vaulted great room featuring a stunning window above the front door
- The vaulted breakfast room is steps from the kitchen island and enjoys covered deck views
- The private master bedroom has direct screened porch access, and a private bath with a roomy walk-in closet
- Off the garage is both a large utility room and a large mud room area filled with storage space
- The optional lower level has an additional 1,787 square feet of living area
- 2-car front entry garage

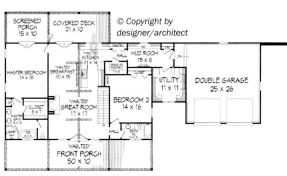

First Floor
1,787 sq. ft.

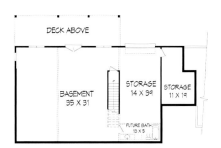

Optional
Lower Level
1,787 sq. ft.

Stylish Patio Designs

Patios and outdoor spaces are usually a "given" with any home design. Homeowners have long insisted their home include a space where they can retreat outdoors for some fresh air. As we have all seen with the current outdoor living trends, the patio space has gone luxury. But, if you still desire something less extravagant, a simple place to relax and unwind after a long workday, then there are some great ideas and materials that can make your special patio a place of enjoyment.

Small patios do not have to be dull or uninteresting. In fact, smaller patios can be the perfect space for sitting, gardening, reading and entertaining. Be sure to start with a solid and seamless material that creates the canvas for the rest of the area and the décor you select.

stylish patio materials for any sized patio

BRICK Easy to install and durable, brick is a timeless material that can easily make your patio match the look and feel of your home. Available in many shades and colors; this is always a popular choice.

STONE OR FLAGSTONE This material is available in pre-cut or random sizes for a natural, rugged look. It can create a rustic feel to the patio and make it appear as if it was always there among nature. It can be an expensive option, but it is long lasting.

STONE VENEER This product has all of the benefits of real stone, but typically is lighter and less expensive.

CONCRETE The most affordable patio material But, like stamped concrete mentioned below, it is easy to add borders for a custom look to your outdoor living space.

STAMPED CONCRETE With this material, homeowners get the look of flagstone, brick and many other materials because they have a stamped pattern pressed into the freshly poured concrete. This is a low-maintenance yet, beautiful option. It can also incorporate brick borders and other designs to give it a more custom look.

PAVERS Man-made and can often look manufactured, but they are easy to install and less expensive than other patio materials.

So, now that you have reviewed the most popular patio materials on the market today, it's time to decide what type of patio surface you should choose. Don't forget to keep in mind the overall look and style of your home. Creating the perfect patio, no matter what the size, is one that matches the interior and exterior of your home. You want this special place to feel like an extension of your interior spaces.

Looking for ways to add style to your patio?

Patio spaces can take on a life of their own when you add a little of your own personality to the area. If you love bold colors, then planting vibrant flowers around the border will liven up the space with color and interest. This is an inexpensive way to add a colorful focal point.

Another great option is durable outdoor furniture. These days, comfortable and durable outdoor furniture can be found just about anywhere. And, most of it is able to withstand the harsh elements a patio will encounter all throughout the year. Since most patios receive full sun and rain exposure, be sure to pick something that is able to withstand many weather changes.

Some stylish accessories that add little expense include wind chimes, fountains and even hammocks. Who wouldn't enjoy falling into a hammock on a perfect summer day in a shady spot right off the patio? This may become the perfect place to relax after mowing the grass, or when reading. And, add in the sound of a water feature, or the sweet sound of wind chimes blowing in the breeze and soon you'll transport yourself to a place of total relaxation. Adding these inexpensive items to your patio will enhance your senses and offer many opportunities for tranquility just steps from your home.

Another popular addition to any patio space is outdoor lighting, which has also become an outdoor staple for many homeowners. Now more than ever, there is little need to worry about outdoor electricity outlets, so why not go solar? Not only is it more economical, but it provides the subtle ambiance that homeowners crave as the sun sets. Plus, it's inexpensive and can be purchased at home improvement retailers all across the country.

While many homeowners are opting for expansive, luxurious patio spaces filled with every amenity, some homeowners have less space to work with and want less maintenance, especially if it's a second home. But that doesn't mean a modest patio space will lack the personality and style their high-end counterparts typical exude. Use some or all of these ideas and soon your cozy patio oasis will be your favorite spot all throughout the year.

Outdoor Dining Ideas

Homeowners have finally started to figure out how to create the perfect atmosphere for outdoor living that incorporates dining, socializing, and even cooking space. Nothing is more relaxing than enjoying good food, and good friends in an outdoor dining space that is totally appealing and equally inviting.

So how do you create such an experience? First, decide what type of area you want. Will the dining area be for entertaining, or do you want an intimate space simply for you and your family? This will give you an idea of how large of a space you need. If you entertain, you will need a large area with enough space for everyone to move about freely.

choose a layout

If you choose a layout for entertaining, remember you will need plenty of room for both sitting and dining. There are a few things to consider when choosing a table. You can choose a table large enough to accommodate all of your typical guests, but a table that size may be a bit overwhelming on a daily basis. Or, choose more than one table or seating arrangement. This creates an intimate dining experience and offers different areas for conversation. If you're looking for a more personal dining experience, a small, intimate table is a suitable choice, or select small tables or position throw cushions around low tables in clusters for a relaxed, casual feel.

choose a material

There are many great dining set options available in wood, metal, wicker, with some now even made from sustainable materials. Look at your home, your patio style, as well as your home's surroundings and decide what style would look best. The look of natural wood fits well with an outdoor space rich in landscaping, or a rustic setting. Wrought iron is popular, elegant, and appropriate for harsh, or windy climates because of its durability and weight. Aluminum dining sets are lightweight and affordable. Metal dining sets are beautiful and durable, but not comfortable without a great cushion. Trendy wicker and rope dining sets are casual and fit nicely with a Modern, or a Modern Farmhouse style home.

Unless noted, all images copyrighted by the designer/architect; Page 88, Top to bottom: Plan #F12-024D-0013 on page 16; Lake view shaded deck, nhmagazine.com, John W. Hession, photographer; patio with candles, istockphoto.com; Plan #101D-0140; Page 89 top: Polywood® Outdoor Furniture featuring Traditional Garden Dining Set, Modern Adirondack Chairs, and 42" Square Fire Pit, polywood.com; Umbrellas add shade and illumination, Design America, photographer; Trex Transcend® Composite Decking, photo courtesy of trex.com; Bottom, left to right: photo from karenkempf.com, article by author Adam Ryan Morris from Milwaukee Magazine ©2012; rope swing with candles, modern-glam.com; See more photos and purchase plans at houseplansandmore.com.

choose sun or shade

Don't overlook sun exposure. No one will be comfortable exposed to excessive sun or heat, so consider adding an umbrella to your patio. Traditional umbrellas stand on a center base with shade given around the perimeter. But, umbrellas also come offset for more room under the umbrella itself. Another option is a retractable awning that rolls out providing shade when needed. Or, add a free standing pergola that offers shade with the permanency of a covered porch. Pergolas are made of wood, wrought iron, or aluminum and can be a fairly simple as a do-it-yourself project, too. If shade is not what you need, then add a dining table with a built-in fire pit and keep family and friends lingering outdoors longer when the temperatures drop.

choose plants & flowers

Also, consider your landscaping when creating a memorable dining spot. Choose welcoming scents from flowers and plants that won't attract unwanted pests or insects. Avoid plants and flowers with unpleasant odors or textures such as thorns or rough leaves and consider plants that actually detract mosquitoes, bees and other unwanted outdoor pests.

choose light & decor

Choosing the perfect lighting can keep the outdoor dining experience going well into the evening. Choose eco-friendly solar lighting and eliminate the need to run wiring, or choose electrical lighting for more options and a brighter light. Last, accessorize with pillows, candles, and fun table settings. These extras add a touch of style and make the area inviting.

Plan #F12-101D-0056

Dimensions:	72' W x 77' D
Heated Sq. Ft.:	2,593
Bonus Sq. Ft.:	1,892
Bedrooms: 2	Bathrooms: 2½
Exterior Walls:	2" x 6"
Foundation:	Walk-out basement

See index for more information

Features

- This stunning home has the look and feel homeowners love with its sleek interior and open floor plan
- The great room, kitchen and dining area combine maximizing the square footage and making these spaces functional and comfortable
- The master bedroom enjoys a first floor location adding convenience for the homeowners
- The optional lower level has an additional 1,892 square feet of living area and adds extra amenities like a media area, billiards space, recreation and exercise rooms, a wet bar, two bedrooms, and two full baths
- 3-car front entry garage

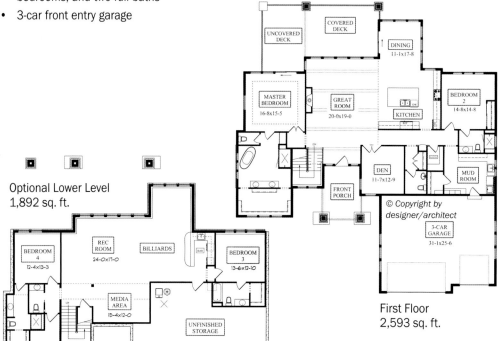

Optional Lower Level
1,892 sq. ft.

© Copyright by
designer/architect

First Floor
2,593 sq. ft.

Images provided by designer/architect

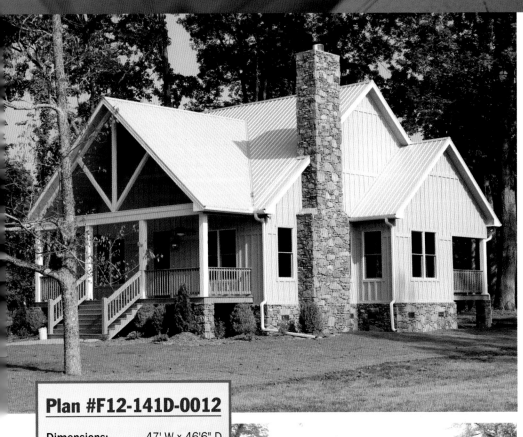

Plan #F12-141D-0012

Dimensions: 47' W x 46'6" D
Heated Sq. Ft.: 1,972
Bedrooms: 3   **Bathrooms:** 3½
Foundation: Crawl space standard; slab, basement or walk-out basement for an additional fee

See index for more information

Features

- An open and airy vaulted family room has a rustic stone fireplace
- The kitchen is completely open to the dining area and the great room making the entire first floor feel spacious and comfortable even when entertaining
- Covered front and back porches create plenty of outdoor living space including the second floor covered porch
- There is a master suite on the first floor as well as two additional master suites on the second floor creating plenty of comfortable living spaces for a live-in parent, or adult child

© Copyright by designer/architect

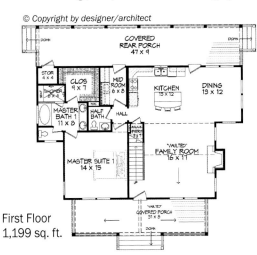

First Floor
1,199 sq. ft.

Second Floor
773 sq. ft.

Images provided by designer/architect

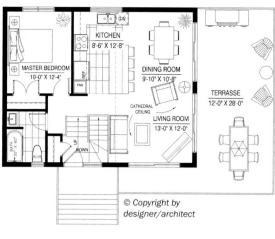

First Floor
720 sq. ft.

KITCHEN
8'-6" X 12'-8"

MASTER BEDROOM
10'-0" X 12'-4"

DINING ROOM
9'-10" X 10'-8"

TERRASSE
12'-0" X 28'-0"

CATHEDRAL CEILING

LIVING ROOM
13'-0" X 12'-0"

BATH 30" X 60"

Plan #F12-148D-0047

Dimensions:	30' W x 24' D
Heated Sq. Ft.:	720
Bonus Sq. Ft.:	720
Bedrooms: 1	Bathrooms: 1
Exterior Walls:	2" x 6"
Foundation:	Basement

See index for more information

Images provided by designer/architect

© Copyright by designer/architect

BEDROOM #2
12'-8" X 10'-0"

BEDROOM #3
10'-0" X 12'-4"

OPTIONAL

SHOWER 36"X48"

BATH 30"X60"

STORAGE

BEDROOM #4/FAMILY ROOM
10'-0" X 10'-0"

CARPORT
12'-0" X 28'-0"

Optional Lower Level
720 sq. ft.

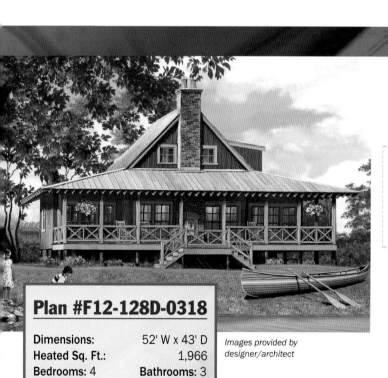

Plan #F12-128D-0318

Dimensions:	52' W x 43' D
Heated Sq. Ft.:	1,966
Bedrooms: 4	Bathrooms: 3
Foundation:	Crawl space

See index for more information

Images provided by designer/architect

Second Floor
548 sq. ft.

© Copyright by designer/architect

OPTIONAL
2 CAR GARAGE
24'-0" X 24'-0"

WALK IN CLOSET

BEDROOM 3
11'-0" X 11'-4"

LINEN

DOWN

BATH 3

BEDROOM 4
14'-0" X 12'-0"

KITCHEN
16'-7" X 10'-10"

BATH 2

PANTRY

DINING
12'-0" X 10'-10"

WALK IN CLOSET

M. BATH

BEDROOM 2
13'-7" X 12'-10"

GREAT ROOM
23'-6" X 17'-6"

MASTER BEDROOM
13'-7" X 13'-0"

GRILLE OR FIREPLACE

PORCH
52'-0" X 13'-4"

First Floor
1,418 sq. ft.

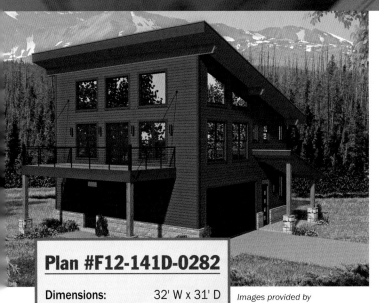

Plan #F12-141D-0282

Dimensions:	32' W x 31' D
Heated Sq. Ft.:	1,359
Bonus Sq. Ft.:	200
Bedrooms: 2	Bathrooms: 2
Exterior Walls:	2" x 6"
Foundation:	Slab

See index for more information

Images provided by designer/architect

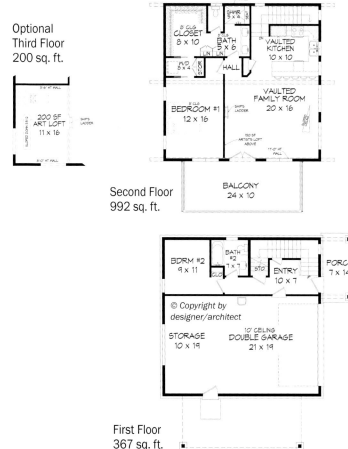

Optional
Third Floor
200 sq. ft.

200 SF
ART LOFT
11 x 16

SHIP'S LADDER

Second Floor
992 sq. ft.

CLOSET 8 x 10

BATH 5 x 6

VAULTED KITCHEN 10 x 10

HALL

BEDROOM #1 12 x 16

SHIP'S LADDER

VAULTED FAMILY ROOM 20 x 16

150 SF ARTIST'S LOFT ABOVE

BALCONY 24 x 10

First Floor
367 sq. ft.

BDRM #2 9 x 11

BATH #2 7 x 7

ENTRY 10 x 7

PORCH 7 x 14

STORAGE 10 x 19

10' CEILING DOUBLE GARAGE 21 x 19

© Copyright by designer/architect

Plan #F12-123D-0264

Dimensions:	34'8" W x 32' D
Heated Sq. Ft.:	733
Bedrooms: 1	Bathrooms: 1

Foundation: Slab standard; crawl space, basement or walk-out basement for an additional fee

See index for more information

Images provided by designer/architect

K. 14 x 8

Grt. Rm. 14 x 16

Br.1 12 x 11

Mech.

Covered Porch

© Copyright by designer/architect

Plan #F12-126D-1029

Dimensions:	24' W x 26' D
Heated Sq. Ft.:	1,036
Bedrooms: 3	Bathrooms: 2
Exterior Walls:	2" x 6"
Foundation:	Basement

See index for more information

Images provided by designer/architect

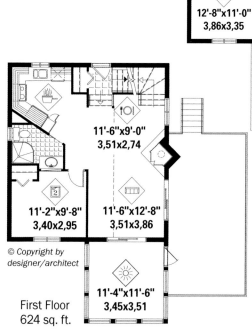

Second Floor
412 sq. ft.

11'-2"x8'-4"
3,40x2,54

12'-8"x11'-0"
3,86x3,35

11'-6"x9'-0"
3,51x2,74

11'-2"x9'-8"
3,40x2,95

11'-6"x12'-8"
3,51x3,86

11'-4"x11'-6"
3,45x3,51

First Floor
624 sq. ft.

Plan #F12-032D-0872

Dimensions:	24' W x 28' D
Heated Sq. Ft.:	629
Bedrooms: 2	Bathrooms: 1
Exterior Walls:	2" x 6"

Foundation: Monolithic slab standard; crawl space or floating slab for an additional fee

See index for more information

Images provided by designer/architect

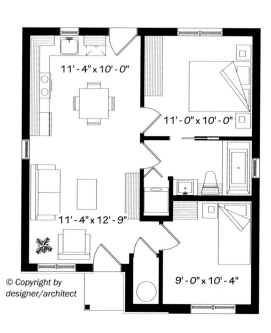

11'- 4" x 10'- 0"

11'- 0" x 10'- 0"

11'- 4" x 12'- 9"

9'- 0" x 10'- 4"

Plan #F12-011D-0660

Dimensions:	52' W x 53' D
Heated Sq. Ft.:	1,704
Bedrooms: 3	Bathrooms: 2½
Exterior Walls:	2" x 6"

Foundation: Crawl space or slab standard; basement for an additional fee

See index for more information

Images provided by designer/architect

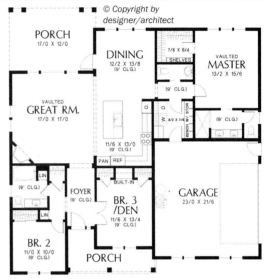

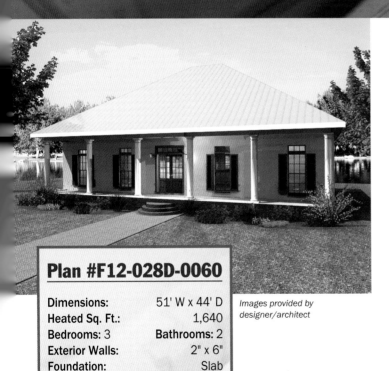

Plan #F12-028D-0060

Dimensions:	51' W x 44' D
Heated Sq. Ft.:	1,640
Bedrooms: 3	Bathrooms: 2
Exterior Walls:	2" x 6"
Foundation:	Slab

See index for more information

Images provided by designer/architect

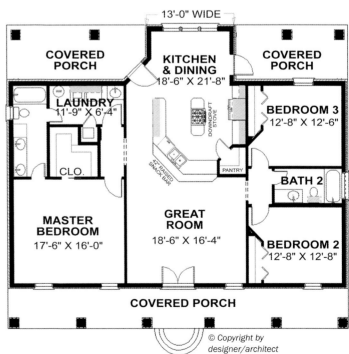

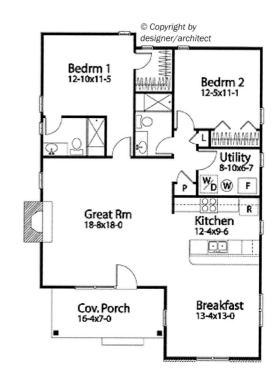

© Copyright by designer/architect

Bedrm 1
12-10x11-5

Bedrm 2
12-5x11-1

Utility
8-10x6-7

Great Rm
18-8x18-0

Kitchen
12-4x9-6

Cov. Porch
16-4x7-0

Breakfast
13-4x13-0

Plan #F12-058D-0243

Dimensions:	34'4" W x 46'4" D
Heated Sq. Ft.:	1,268
Bedrooms: 2	Bathrooms: 2
Foundation:	Slab

See index for more information

Images provided by designer/architect

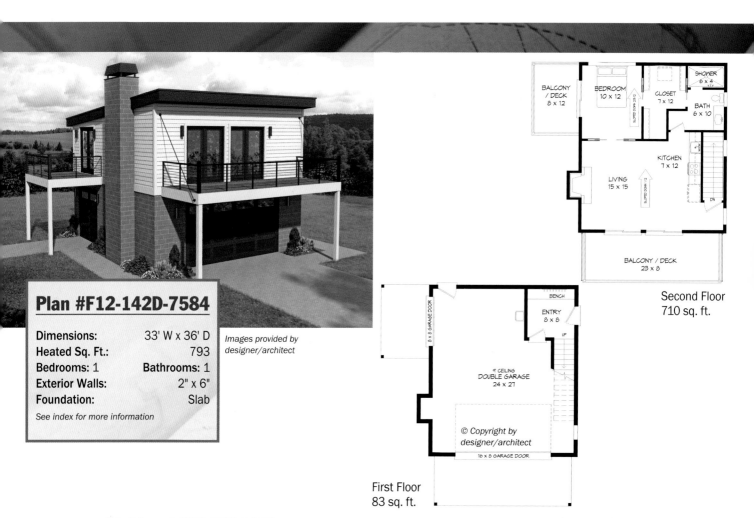

BALCONY / DECK
8 x 12

BEDROOM
10 x 12

CLOSET
7 x 12

SHOWER
6 x 4

BATH
6 x 10

KITCHEN
7 x 12

LIVING
15 x 15

BALCONY / DECK
23 x 8

Second Floor
710 sq. ft.

BENCH

ENTRY
8 x 8

9' CEILING
DOUBLE GARAGE
24 x 27

8 X 8 GARAGE DOOR

16 X 8 GARAGE DOOR

© Copyright by designer/architect

First Floor
83 sq. ft.

Plan #F12-142D-7584

Dimensions:	33' W x 36' D
Heated Sq. Ft.:	793
Bedrooms: 1	Bathrooms: 1
Exterior Walls:	2" x 6"
Foundation:	Slab

See index for more information

Images provided by designer/architect

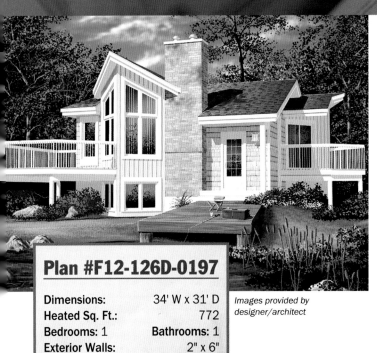

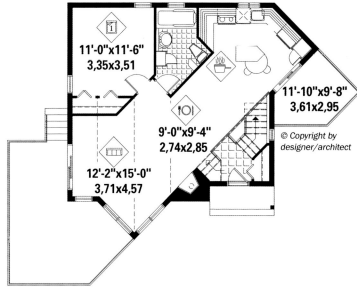

11'-0"x11'-6"
3,35x3,51

11'-10"x9'-8"
3,61x2,95

9'-0"x9'-4"
2,74x2,85

12'-2"x15'-0"
3,71x4,57

© Copyright by
designer/architect

Images provided by
designer/architect

Plan #F12-126D-0197

Dimensions:	34' W x 31' D
Heated Sq. Ft.:	772
Bedrooms: 1	Bathrooms: 1
Exterior Walls:	2" x 6"
Foundation:	Basement

See index for more information

Plan #F12-156D-0014

Dimensions:	25' W x 28' D
Heated Sq. Ft.:	551
Bedrooms: 1	Bathrooms: 1
Foundation:	Slab

See index for more information

Images provided by
designer/architect

BEDROOM
10'-5" X 9'

CLO.
2' X 5'-5"

BATH
9'-2" X 7'-7"

W/D

HALL
4'-1" X 5'-6"

LINENS
3'-7" X 1'-10"

UTIL
3'-2" X 3'-4"

KITCHEN
12'-7" X 10'-5"

LIVING
11'-9" X 11'-9"

Raised clg. - 10'

CLO.
2'-4" X 2'-4"

PORCH
8'-11" X 4'-10"

© Copyright by
designer/architect

Plan #F12-141D-0021

Dimensions: 33'4" W x 46' D
Heated Sq. Ft.: 1,267
Bedrooms: 2 **Bathrooms:** 2
Foundation: Pier standard; slab, crawl space, basement or walk-out basement for an additional fee

See index for more information

Images provided by designer/architect

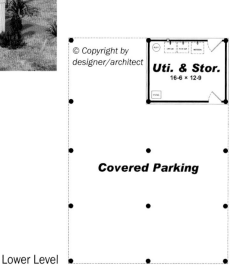

© Copyright by designer/architect

Uti. & Stor.
16-6 × 12-9

Covered Parking

Lower Level

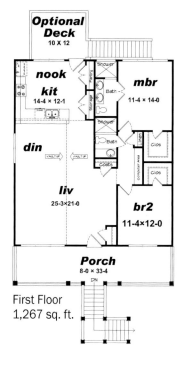

Optional Deck
10 X 12

nook
kit
14-4 × 12-1

din

liv
25-3×21-0

mbr
11-4 × 14-0

br2
11-4×12-0

Porch
8-0 × 33-4

First Floor
1,267 sq. ft.

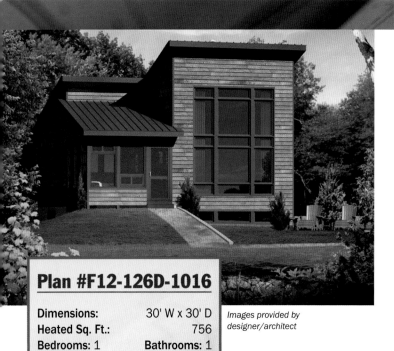

Plan #F12-126D-1016

Dimensions: 30' W x 30' D
Heated Sq. Ft.: 756
Bedrooms: 1 **Bathrooms:** 1
Exterior Walls: 2" x 6"
Foundation: Basement

See index for more information

Images provided by designer/architect

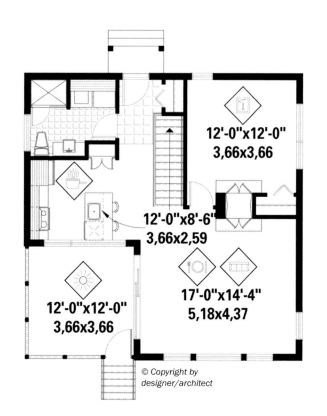

12'-0"x12'-0"
3,66x3,66

12'-0"x8'-6"
3,66x2,59

12'-0"x12'-0"
3,66x3,66

17'-0"x14'-4"
5,18x4,37

© Copyright by designer/architect

Second Floor
572 sq. ft.

Plan #F12-141D-0461

Dimensions: 46' W x 52' D
Heated Sq. Ft.: 2,061
Bonus Sq. Ft.: 681
Bedrooms: 2   **Bathrooms:** 2½
Foundation: Walk-out basement standard; crawl space, slab or walk-out basement for an additional fee

See index for more information

Images provided by designer/architect

Optional
Lower Level
681 sq. ft.

FUTURE BATH 8 x 12
FUTURE BONUS 31 x 13
KITCHENETTE 13 x 4
MECH 8 x 11
2-CAR GARAGE 31 x 22

© Copyright by designer/architect

First Floor
1,489 sq. ft.

CLOSET 10 x 12
PET ROOM 6 x 6
MASTER BATH 11 x 12
MASTER BEDROOM 18 x 13
COVERED DECK 6 x 18
LAUNDRY 13 x 6
1/2 BATH 5 x 5
MUDROOM 8 x 5
"VAULTED" KITCHEN 14 x 10
COVERED DECK 8 x 7
"VAULTED" GREAT ROOM 18 x 22
DECK 6 x 22
DECK 6 x 9
"VAULTED" DINING 13 x 12
DECK 44 x 12

Plan #F12-008D-0162

Dimensions: 26' W x 36' D
Heated Sq. Ft.: 865
Bedrooms: 2   **Bathrooms:** 1
Foundation: Pier

See index for more information

Images provided by designer/architect

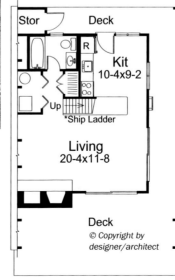

Stor
Deck
Kit 10-4x9-2
R
Up
*Ship Ladder
Living 20-4x11-8
Deck

© Copyright by designer/architect

First Floor
495 sq. ft.

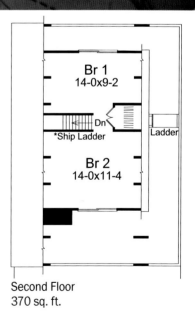

Br 1 14-0x9-2
Dn
*Ship Ladder
Ladder
Br 2 14-0x11-4

Second Floor
370 sq. ft.

Plan #F12-161D-0001

Dimensions:	145'9" W x 93' D
Heated Sq. Ft.:	4,036
Bedrooms: 3	**Bathrooms:** 3½
Exterior Walls:	2" x 8"

Foundation: Crawl space or slab, please specify when ordering

See index for more information

Features

- Craftsman and modern style collide with this stunning rustic one-story home
- The open floor plan is ideal for maximizing square footage
- The master suite can be found in its own wing and it features a huge bath and two walk-in closets
- Built-ins and a walk-in pantry keep the kitchen sleek and clutter-free
- There is a flex space perfect as a kid's playroom
- 3-car side entry garage

Images provided by designer/architect

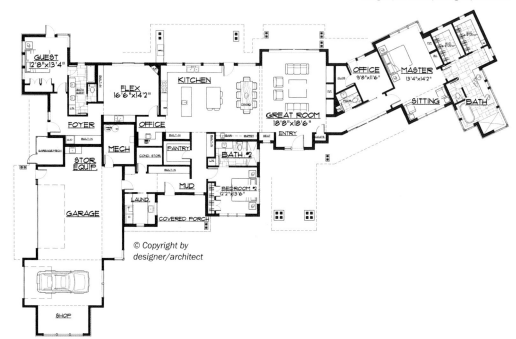

© Copyright by designer/architect

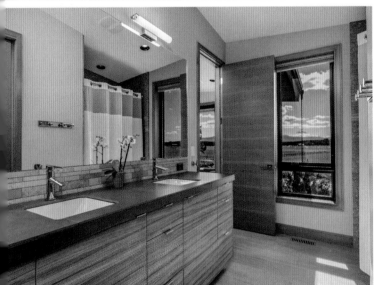

Plan #F12-019D-0048

Dimensions: 89'3" W x 48'8" D
Heated Sq. Ft.: 2,248
Bedrooms: 3   **Bathrooms:** 2
Foundation: Slab standard; crawl space or basement for an additional fee

See index for more information

Images provided by designer/architect

© Copyright by designer/architect

Plan #F12-122D-0001

Dimensions: 33' W x 35' D
Heated Sq. Ft.: 1,105
Bedrooms: 2   **Bathrooms:** 1½
Foundation: Slab

See index for more information

Images provided by designer/architect

Second Floor
225 sq. ft.

First Floor
880 sq. ft.

© Copyright by designer/architect

Plan #F12-020D-0397

Dimensions: 59' W x 50' D
Heated Sq. Ft.: 1,608
Bedrooms: 3 **Bathrooms:** 2
Exterior Walls: 2" x 6"
Foundation: Crawl space standard; slab for an additional fee

See index for more information

Images provided by designer/architect

© Copyright by designer/architect

Plan #F12-058D-0197

Dimensions: 35' W x 30'8" D
Heated Sq. Ft.: 781
Bedrooms: 1 **Bathrooms:** 1
Foundation: Crawl space

See index for more information

Images provided by designer/architect

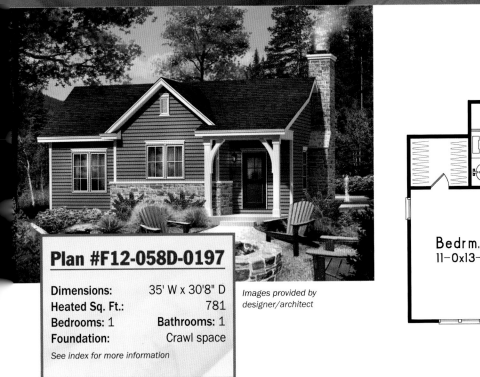

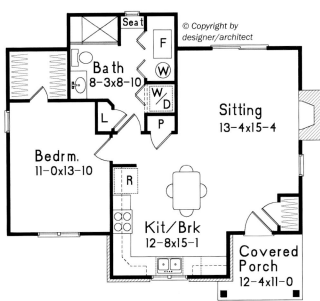

© Copyright by designer/architect

Plan #F12-144D-0024

Dimensions: 32' W x 32' D
Heated Sq. Ft.: 1,024
Bedrooms: 1 **Bathrooms:** 1½
Exterior Walls: 2" x 6"
Foundation: Crawl space or slab standard; basement or walk-out basement for an additional fee
See index for more information

Images provided by designer/architect

© Copyright by designer/architect

LAUNDRY

WALK IN CLOSET
11' 5" x 6' 6"

KITCHEN
13' 2" x 12' 4"

ENSUITE

ROLL-IN SHOWER

PANTRY
5' 11" x 7' 0"

CLOSET

ENTRY

POWDER

LIVING ROOM
13' 0" x 14' 10"

MASTER BEDROOM
11' 5" x 17' 5"

Plan #F12-141D-0479

Dimensions: 68' W x 50' D
Heated Sq. Ft.: 1,740
Bonus Sq. Ft.: 1,740
Bedrooms: 2 **Bathrooms:** 2
Foundation: Walk-out basement standard; crawl space, slab or basement for an additional fee
See index for more information

Images provided by designer/architect

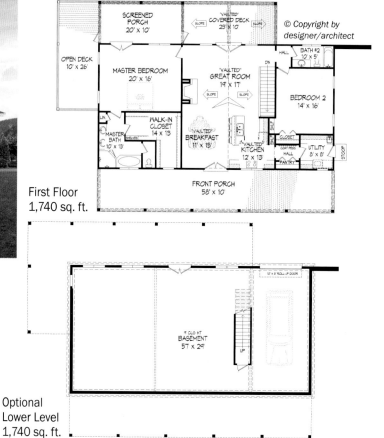

© Copyright by designer/architect

SCREENED PORCH
20' x 10'

'VAULTED' COVERED DECK
25' x 10'

SLOPE

OPEN DECK
10' x 26'

MASTER BEDROOM
20' 16'

'VAULTED' GREAT ROOM
19' x 17'

SLOPE

HALL

BATH #2
10' x 5'

DN

BEDROOM 2
14' x 16'

WALK-IN CLOSET
14' x 13'

MASTER BATH
10' x 13'

'VAULTED' BREAKFAST
11' x 15'

'VAULTED' KITCHEN
12' x 13'

CLOSET

COAT PEGS

HALL PANTRY

UTILITY
8' x 8'

STOOP

FRONT PORCH
58' x 10'

First Floor
1,740 sq. ft.

10' x 8' ROLL-UP DOOR

9' CLG HT BASEMENT
57' x 29'

UP

Optional Lower Level
1,740 sq. ft.

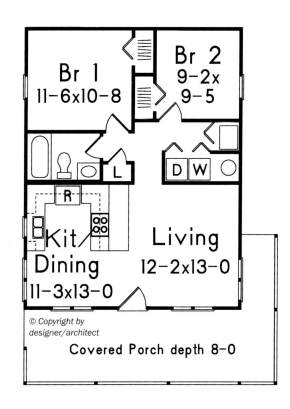

Plan #F12-001D-0085

Dimensions:	28' W x 38' D
Heated Sq. Ft.:	720
Bedrooms: 2	Bathrooms: 1

Foundation: Crawl space standard;
slab for an additional fee

See index for more information

Images provided by designer/architect

Br 1
11-6x10-8

Br 2
9-2x
9-5

L

D W

Kit/
Dining
11-3x13-0

R

Living
12-2x13-0

© Copyright by designer/architect

Covered Porch depth 8-0

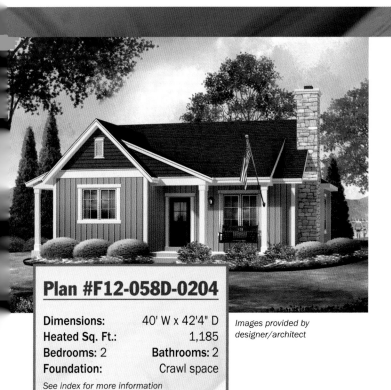

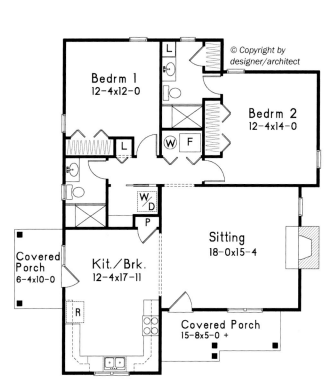

Plan #F12-058D-0204

Dimensions:	40' W x 42'4" D
Heated Sq. Ft.:	1,185
Bedrooms: 2	Bathrooms: 2
Foundation:	Crawl space

See index for more information

Images provided by designer/architect

© Copyright by designer/architect

Bedrm 1
12-4x12-0

L

Bedrm 2
12-4x14-0

L

W F

W/D

P

Covered
Porch
6-4x10-0

Kit./Brk.
12-4x17-11

Sitting
18-0x15-4

R

Covered Porch
15-8x5-0 +

Plan #F12-051D-0970

Dimensions:	37' W x 68' D
Heated Sq. Ft.:	1,354
Bedrooms: 2	**Bathrooms:** 2
Exterior Walls:	2" x 6"

Foundation: Basement standard; crawl space or slab for an additional fee

See index for more information

Features

- Small and stylish, this home offers the layout everyone loves in an easy-to-maintain size
- The covered front porch is large enough for relaxing, while the rear has a screened porch with access onto an open deck, perfect when grilling
- The private master bedroom has a private bath with an oversized walk-in shower, a double-bowl vanity, and a spacious walk-in closet
- Bedroom 2 is just steps away from a full bath
- 2-car front entry garage

Images provided by designer/architect

Plan #F12-141D-0025

Dimensions: 45' W x 50'10" D
Heated Sq. Ft.: 2,033
Bedrooms: 2 **Bathrooms:** 2
Foundation: Crawl space standard; slab, basement or walk-out basement for an additional fee

See index for more information

Features

- Relax in style in this casual vaulted home featuring a family room with a cozy fireplace as a focal point

Images provided by designer/architect

- The kitchen island is double-sided with casual dining space creating a great place for dining, or pull the chairs away and use for a food preparation area, or for serving buffet-style meals
- The second floor is an open loft that can be used as an office or extra sleeping space
- The vaulted outdoor porch is great for grilling

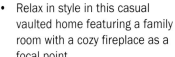
First Floor
1,478 sq. ft.

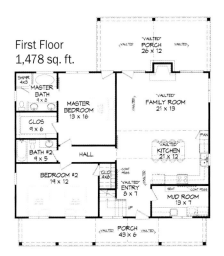

Second Floor
555 sq. ft.

© Copyright by designer/architect

Plan #F12-141D-0233

Dimensions: 38'2" W x 38'6" D
Heated Sq. Ft.: 1,835
Bonus Sq. Ft.: 600
Bedrooms: 3   **Bathrooms:** 2½
Foundation: Basement standard; crawl space, slab or walk-out basement for an additional fee

See index for more information

Images provided by designer/architect

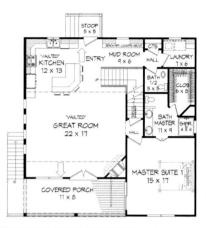

Second Floor
546 sq. ft.

© Copyright by designer/architect

Optional Lower Level
600 sq. ft.

First Floor
1,289 sq. ft.

Plan #F12-126D-1003

Dimensions: 24' W x 26' D
Heated Sq. Ft.: 624
Bedrooms: 1   **Bathrooms:** 1
Exterior Walls: 2" x 6"
Foundation: Basement

See index for more information

Images provided by designer/architect

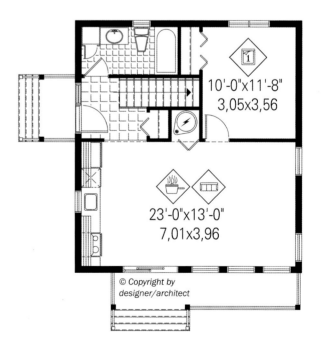

10'-0"x11'-8"
3,05x3,56

23'-0"x13'-0"
7,01x3,96

© Copyright by designer/architect

Plan #F12-163D-0013

Dimensions:	52' W x 40' D
Heated Sq. Ft.:	1,676
Bedrooms: 3	Bathrooms: 3
Exterior Walls:	2" x 6"

Foundation: Crawl space or slab, please specify when ordering

See index for more information

Images provided by designer/architect

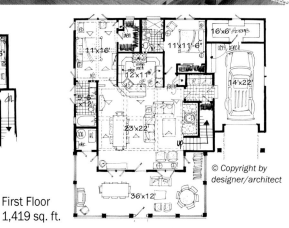

Second Floor
257 sq. ft.

First Floor
1,419 sq. ft.

© Copyright by designer/architect

Plan #F12-008D-0133

Dimensions:	26' W x 24' D
Heated Sq. Ft.:	624
Bedrooms: 2	Bathrooms: 1
Foundation:	Pier

See index for more information

Images provided by designer/architect

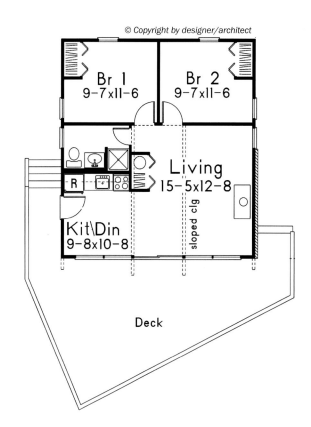

© Copyright by designer/architect

Br 1
9-7x11-6

Br 2
9-7x11-6

Living
15-5x12-8
sloped clg

Kit\Din
9-8x10-8

R

Deck

Plan #F12-163D-0003

Dimensions:	56' W x 40' D
Heated Sq. Ft.:	1,416
Bedrooms: 3	Bathrooms: 2
Exterior Walls:	2" x 6"
Foundation:	Crawl space

See index for more information

Images provided by designer/architect

Features

- Covered front and back porches are large enough to enjoy the outdoors in comfort
- The great room is open to both the kitchen and dining area on the left side of the house for an open, airy feel
- All three bedrooms are located on the right side of the house with the master suite having a private sitting porch in the back
- The laundry room is conveniently located just off of the kitchen

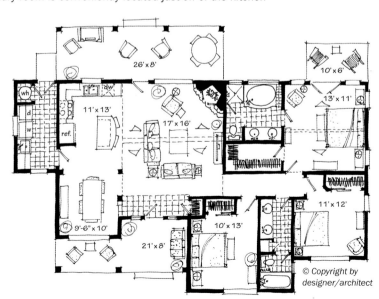

© Copyright by designer/architect

Plan #F12-024S-0021

Dimensions:	80' W x 66' D
Heated Sq. Ft.:	5,862
Bedrooms: 6	Bathrooms: 5

Foundation: Basement or pier, please specify when ordering

See index for more information

Features

- Decorative columns line the perimeter of the formal dining room for an elegant, open feel
- The family room enjoys a vaulted ceiling for a spacious atmosphere
- The master bedroom features a private sitting area that leads to the covered porch
- One of the second floor bedrooms has direct access to a private balcony
- This plan features an above ground basement option
- 3-car drive under side entry garage

Second Floor
901 sq. ft.

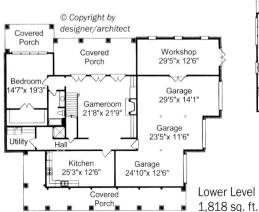

© Copyright by designer/architect

Lower Level
1,818 sq. ft.

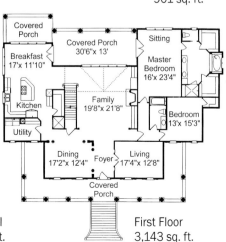

First Floor
3,143 sq. ft.

Images provided by designer/architect

Plan #F12-126D-1012

Dimensions:	30' W x 30' D
Heated Sq. Ft.:	815
Bedrooms: 1	Bathrooms: 1
Exterior Walls:	2" x 6"
Foundation:	Basement

See index for more information

Images provided by designer/architect

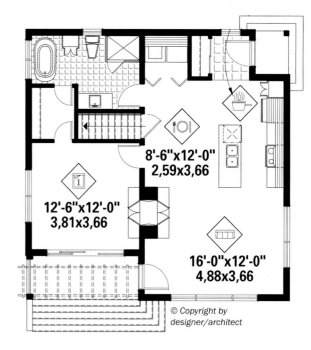

8'-6"x12'-0"
2,59x3,66

12'-6"x12'-0"
3,81x3,66

16'-0"x12'-0"
4,88x3,66

© Copyright by designer/architect

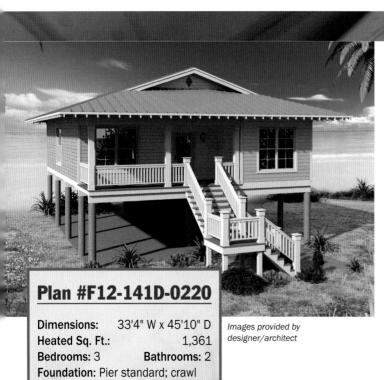

Plan #F12-141D-0220

Dimensions:	33'4" W x 45'10" D
Heated Sq. Ft.:	1,361
Bedrooms: 3	Bathrooms: 2

Foundation: Pier standard; crawl space, slab, basement or walk-out basement for an additional fee

See index for more information

Images provided by designer/architect

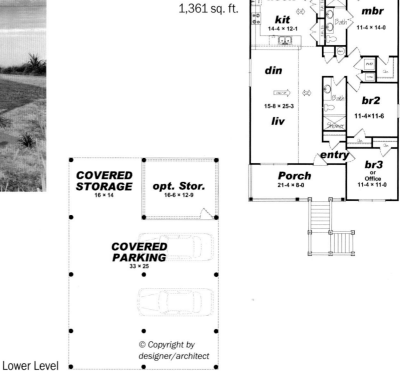

First Floor
1,361 sq. ft.

DECK
33-4 × 11-11

nook

kit
14-4 × 12-1

mbr
11-4 × 14-0

din

15-8 × 25-3

br2
11-4×11-6

liv

Bath

Shower

entry

Porch
21-4 × 8-0

br3
or
Office
11-4 × 11-0

COVERED STORAGE
16 × 14

opt. Stor.
16-6 × 12-9

COVERED PARKING
33 × 25

Lower Level

© Copyright by designer/architect

Plan #F12-058D-0238

Dimensions:	40'4" W x 48' D
Heated Sq. Ft.:	1,149
Bedrooms: 3	Bathrooms: 2
Foundation:	Basement

See index for more information

Images provided by designer/architect

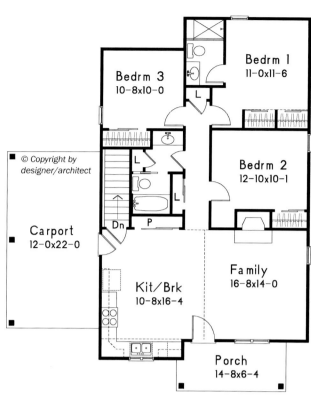

© Copyright by designer/architect

Bedrm 3
10-8x10-0

Bedrm 1
11-0x11-6

Bedrm 2
12-10x10-1

Carport
12-0x22-0

Kit/Brk
10-8x16-4

Family
16-8x14-0

Porch
14-8x6-4

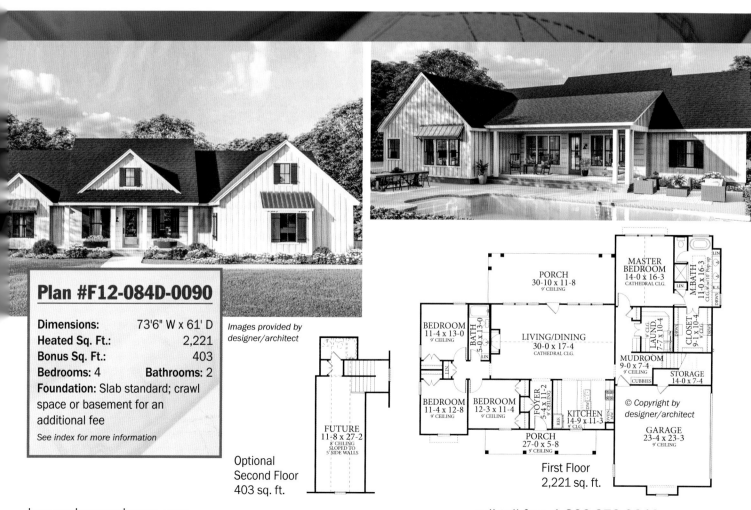

Plan #F12-084D-0090

Dimensions:	73'6" W x 61' D
Heated Sq. Ft.:	2,221
Bonus Sq. Ft.:	403
Bedrooms: 4	Bathrooms: 2
Foundation:	Slab standard; crawl space or basement for an additional fee

See index for more information

Images provided by designer/architect

FUTURE
11-8 x 27-2
8' CEILING
SLOPED TO
5' SIDE WALLS

Optional
Second Floor
403 sq. ft.

PORCH
30-10 x 11-8
9' CEILING

MASTER
BEDROOM
14-0 x 16-3
CATHEDRAL CLG.

M.BATH
11-0 x 16-3
CLG.9'w/10' Pop-up

BEDROOM
11-4 x 13-0
9' CEILING

BATH
5-0 x 13-0

LIVING/DINING
30-0 x 17-4
CATHEDRAL CLG.

LAUND.
7-7 x 10-4

CLOSET
9-1 x 10-4

BEDROOM
11-4 x 12-8
9' CEILING

BEDROOM
12-3 x 11-4
9' CEILING

FOYER
5-4 x 11-2
9' CEILING

KITCHEN
14-9 x 11-3
9' CLG.

MUDROOM
9-0 x 7-4
9' CEILING

CUBBIES

STORAGE
14-0 x 7-4

© Copyright by designer/architect

PORCH
27-0 x 5-8
9' CEILING

GARAGE
23-4 x 23-3
9' CEILING

First Floor
2,221 sq. ft.

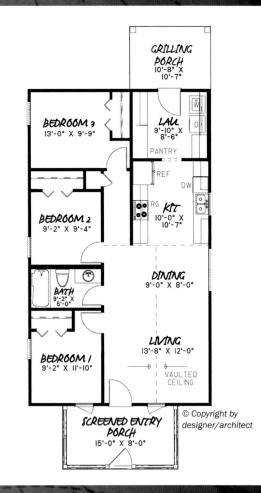

GRILLING PORCH
10'-8" X 10'-7"

BEDROOM 3
13'-0" X 9'-9"

LAU
9'-10" X 8'-6"

PANTRY

REF

DW

BEDROOM 2
9'-2" X 9'-4"

KIT
10'-0" X 10'-7"

RG

BATH
9'-2" X 5'-0"

DINING
9'-0" X 8'-0"

BEDROOM 1
9'-2" X 11'-10"

LIVING
13'-8" X 12'-0"

VAULTED CEILING

SCREENED ENTRY PORCH
15'-0" X 8'-0"

© Copyright by designer/architect

Plan #F12-155D-0100

Dimensions: 24' W x 56'6" D
Heated Sq. Ft.: 970
Bedrooms: 3   Bathrooms: 1
Foundation: Crawl space or slab, please specify when ordering

See index for more information

Images provided by designer/architect

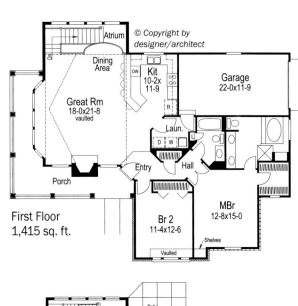

Atrium

© Copyright by designer/architect

Dining Area

Kit
10-2x 11-9

Garage
22-0x11-9

Great Rm
18-0x21-8
vaulted

DW

R

Laun.

Entry

Hall

Porch

MBr
12-8x15-0

Br 2
11-4x12-6

Shelves

Vaulted

First Floor
1,415 sq. ft.

Up

Patio

Family Rm
25-0x21-4

Unexcavated

Lower Level
507 sq. ft.

Unfinished Basement

Plan #F12-007D-0068

Dimensions: 55'8" W x 46'4" D
Heated Sq. Ft.: 1,922
Bedrooms: 2   Bathrooms: 2
Foundation: Walk-out basement

See index for more information

Images provided by designer/architect

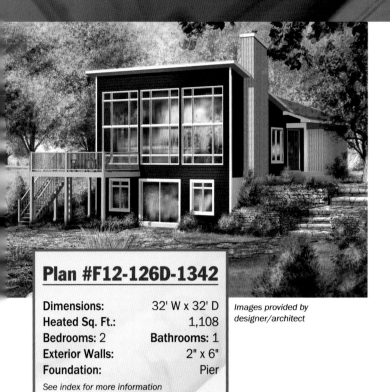

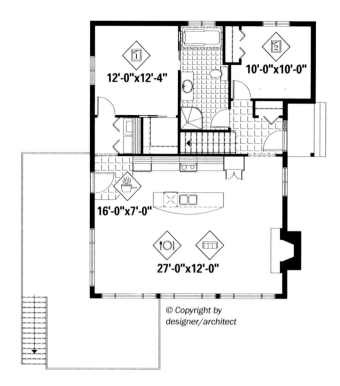

Plan #F12-126D-1342

Dimensions:	32' W x 32' D
Heated Sq. Ft.:	1,108
Bedrooms: 2	Bathrooms: 1
Exterior Walls:	2" x 6"
Foundation:	Pier

See index for more information

Images provided by designer/architect

12'-0"x12'-4"

10'-0"x10'-0"

16'-0"x7'-0"

27'-0"x12'-0"

© Copyright by designer/architect

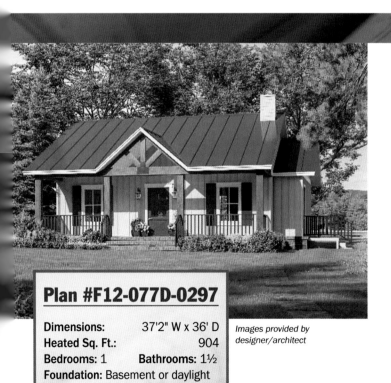

Plan #F12-077D-0297

Dimensions:	37'2" W x 36' D
Heated Sq. Ft.:	904
Bedrooms: 1	Bathrooms: 1½

Foundation: Basement or daylight basement standard; for crawl space or slab versions, see Plan #077D-0296 at houseplansanmore.com

See index for more information

Images provided by designer/architect

Seat
4x6 Shower
Bath 12-2 x 6
Laundry 5-6 x 5-2
Rear Porch 9-10 x 4-4
Storage 4-2 x 4-0

Half Bath 5-8 x 5-2
Eat-In Kitchen 13-6 x 10-8 9' Clg. Ht.
Stairs To Basement

Bedroom 12-2 x 14-2 9' Clg. Ht.
Pantry 5-9 x 3-10
ATTIC ACCESS
Down

VAULT

Living Room 19-6 X 12 Vaulted Clg.
Side Entry 4-2 x 7-2
Bench

Closet 8-10 x 6-4
HVAC
Closet
Wood Burning Fireplace
Shelves
VAULT

Front Porch 32-8 x 8
VAULT
VAULT

© Copyright by designer/architect

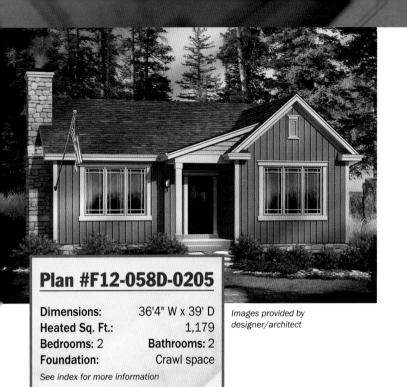

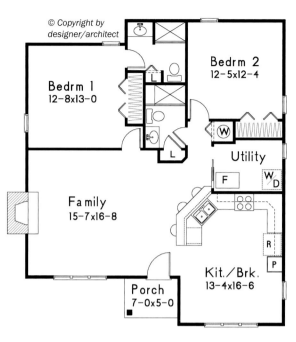

Plan #F12-058D-0205

Dimensions:	36'4" W x 39' D
Heated Sq. Ft.:	1,179
Bedrooms: 2	Bathrooms: 2
Foundation:	Crawl space

See index for more information

Images provided by designer/architect

© Copyright by designer/architect

Bedrm 1
12-8x13-0

Bedrm 2
12-5x12-4

L

W

Utility

F

W D

Family
15-7x16-8

Kit./Brk.
13-4x16-6

R

P

Porch
7-0x5-0

Plan #F12-011D-0307

Dimensions:	40' W x 57' D
Heated Sq. Ft.:	1,529
Bedrooms: 3	Bathrooms: 2
Exterior Walls:	2" x 6"

Foundation: Crawl space or slab standard; basement for an additional fee

See index for more information

Images provided by designer/architect

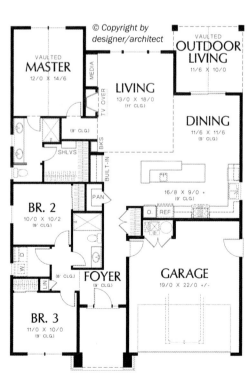

© Copyright by designer/architect

VAULTED
MASTER
12/0 X 14/6

MEDIA

TV OVER

VAULTED
OUTDOOR
LIVING
11/6 X 10/0

LIVING
13/0 X 18/0
(11' CLG.)

DINING
11/6 X 11/6
(9' CLG.)

(9' CLG.)

SHLVS

BKS

BUILT-IN

BR. 2
10/0 X 10/2
(9' CLG.)

PAN

16/8 X 9/0 +
(9' CLG.)

O.

REF

W D

(8' CLG.)

LIN

FOYER
(9' CLG.)

GARAGE
19/0 X 22/0 +/-

BR. 3
11/0 X 10/0
(9' CLG.)

Plan #F12-026D-2035

Dimensions: 40' W x 50'8" D
Heated Sq. Ft.: 2,597
Bedrooms: 4 **Bathrooms:** 3½
Exterior Walls: 2" x 6"
Foundation: Basement standard; crawl space, slab or walk-out basement for an additional fee

See index for more information

Images provided by designer/architect

© Copyright by designer/architect

Second Floor
1,497 sq. ft.

First Floor
1,100 sq. ft.

Plan #F12-032D-1076

Dimensions: 54' W x 42' D
Heated Sq. Ft.: 2,146
Bedrooms: 4 **Bathrooms:** 3
Exterior Walls: 2" x 6"
Foundation: Crawl space standard; monolithic slab or floating slab for an additional fee

See index for more information

Images provided by designer/architect

© Copyright by designer/architect

Front View

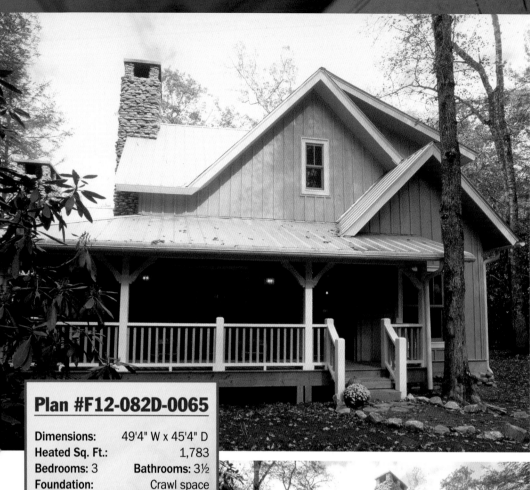

Plan #F12-082D-0065

Dimensions: 49'4" W x 45'4" D
Heated Sq. Ft.: 1,783
Bedrooms: 3   **Bathrooms:** 3½
Foundation: Crawl space

See index for more information

Features

- Enter into the family room that gives a warm welcome with its stone fireplace and open railing
- The beautiful screened porch boasts a rustic vaulted wood beam ceiling and a cozy fireplace
- The kitchen is open to the dining area and has a narrow center island adding valuable workspace without compromising room to move around
- The master bath has a spacious glass shower, an oversized spa tub, a double-bowl vanity, and a separate toilet

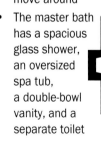

Images provided by designer/architect

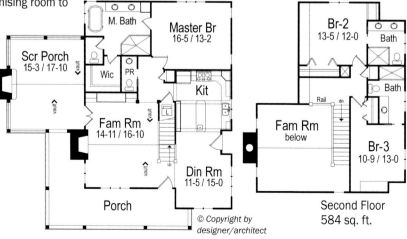

First Floor
1,199 sq. ft.

Second Floor
584 sq. ft.

© Copyright by designer/architect

Plan #F12-032D-0709

Dimensions: 24' W x 20' D
Heated Sq. Ft.: 480
Bedrooms: 2 **Bathrooms:** 1
Exterior Walls: 2" x 6"
Foundation: Screw pile standard; crawl space, floating slab or monolithic slab for an additional fee

See index for more information

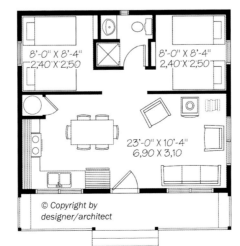

Features

- This terrific cottage/cabin style home is the perfect design featuring plenty of windows for added sunlight and a covered front porch adding great curb appeal
- There is one main room that combines the living and dining area together with the kitchen nearby
- The bedroom is large enough for several beds making it perfect for a vacation getaway
- In order to respect the building code and also meet the multiple needs of customers, when this plan is ordered you will have two versions of the cottage design included
- The first version includes an uninsulated and unheated version for seasonal use only (3 seasons) with 2" x 4" walls, 2" x 8" floor joists, and 2" x 8" roof rafters
- The second version is an insulated and heated version for permanent occupation (4 seasons) with 2" x 6" walls, 2" x 10" floor joists, and the roof designed with roof trusses
- Both versions are provided on screw piles to ensure stability

8'-0" X 8'-4"
2,40 X 2,50

8'-0" X 8'-4"
2,40 X 2,50

23'-0" X 10'-4"
6,90 X 3,10

© Copyright by designer/architect

Images provided by designer/architect

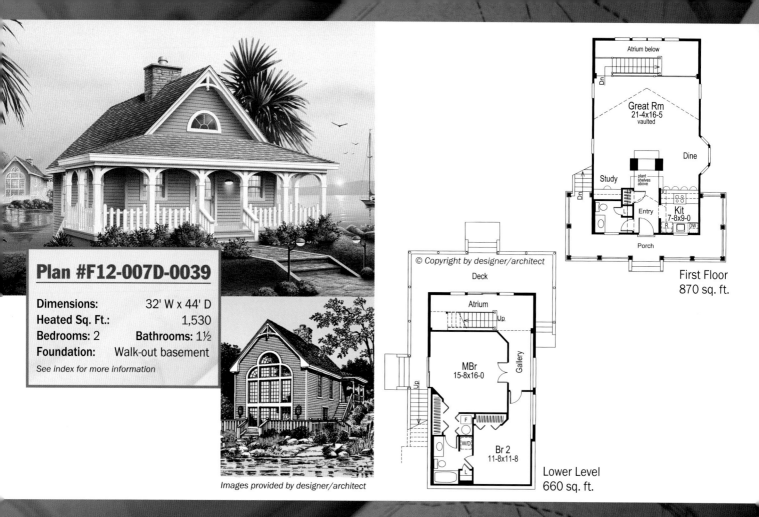

Plan #F12-007D-0039

Dimensions: 32' W x 44' D
Heated Sq. Ft.:   1,530
Bedrooms: 2   Bathrooms: 1½
Foundation: Walk-out basement

See index for more information

Images provided by designer/architect

© Copyright by designer/architect

First Floor
870 sq. ft.

Great Rm
21-4x16-5
vaulted

Dine

Study

plant shelves above

Entry

Kit
7-8x9-0

Porch

Atrium below

Dn

Deck

Atrium

Up

MBr
15-8x16-0

Gallery

Up

F

W/D

Br 2
11-8x11-8

Lower Level
660 sq. ft.

Plan #F12-121D-0023

Dimensions: 41' W x 60'4" D
Heated Sq. Ft.:   1,762
Bedrooms: 3   Bathrooms: 2
Foundation: Basement standard;
crawl space or slab for an
additional fee

See index for more information

*Images provided by
designer/architect*

Patio

MBr
15-0x16-11
Vaulted
Opt Coffer

Kit
12-8x14-9
Vaulted

Dining
12-4x12-9
Vaulted

Great Rm
18-8x16-11
Vaulted

Laun/ Mud Rm

Dn

Garage
21-4x20-0

Entry

Br 2
10-11x12-2

© Copyright by
designer/architect

Porch

Br 3
10-11x11-9

Plan #F12-001D-0031

Dimensions:	48' W x 66' D
Heated Sq. Ft.:	1,501
Bedrooms: 3	**Bathrooms:** 2

Foundation: Basement standard; crawl space or slab for an additional fee

See index for more information

Images provided by designer/architect

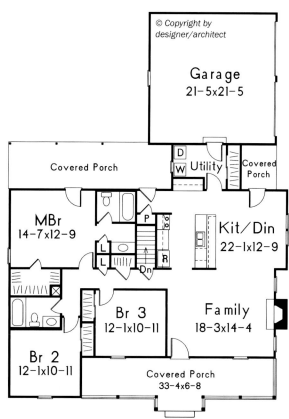

Garage
21-5x21-5

Covered Porch

Utility

Covered Porch

MBr
14-7x12-9

Kit/Din
22-1x12-9

Br 3
12-1x10-11

Family
18-3x14-4

Br 2
12-1x10-11

Covered Porch
33-4x6-8

Plan #F12-011D-0683

Dimensions:	17' W x 41' D
Heated Sq. Ft.:	944
Bedrooms: 2	**Bathrooms:** 1½
Exterior Walls:	2" x 6"

Foundation: Crawl space or slab standard; basement for an additional fee

See index for more information

Images provided by designer/architect

T.W.H

REF

8/0 X 9/0
(9' CLG.)

SHLVS

PAN

BR. 2
11/6 X 10/0
(8' CLG.)

W/D

LIN

DN.

LIV/DIN
11/6 X 20/0
(9' CLG.)

STOR

UP

BR. 1
11/6 X 10/0
(8' CLG.)

First Floor
489 sq. ft.

SEAT

PORCH

Second Floor
455 sq. ft.

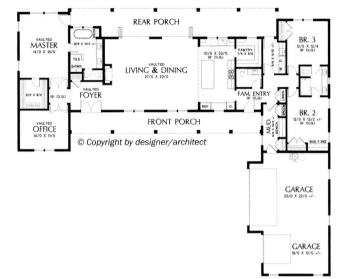

© Copyright by designer/architect

REAR PORCH

VAULTED MASTER
14/0 X 18/0

TILE
SHWR

VAULTED LIVING & DINING
27/0 X 20/0

10/0 X 20/0
(9' CLG.)

PANTRY
7/4 X 6/0

BR. 3
12/0 X 12/4
(9' CLG.)

VAULTED FOYER

VAULTED OFFICE
14/0 X 11/0

FAM. ENTRY
(9' CLG.)

REF

FRONT PORCH

MUD.

BR. 2
12/0 X 13/2
(9' CLG.)

BUILT-INS

GARAGE
23/0 X 22/0 +/-

GARAGE
19/0 X 12/0 +/-

Plan #F12-011D-0630

Images provided by designer/architect

Dimensions: 90' W x 75' D
Heated Sq. Ft.: 2,495
Bedrooms: 3   **Bathrooms:** 2½
Exterior Walls: 2" x 6"
Foundation: Crawl space or slab standard; basement for an additional fee

See index for more information

© Copyright by designer/architect

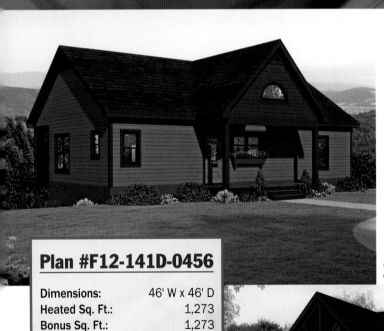

Plan #F12-141D-0456

Dimensions: 46' W x 46' D
Heated Sq. Ft.: 1,273
Bonus Sq. Ft.: 1,273
Bedrooms: 3   **Bathrooms:** 2
Exterior Walls: 2" x 6"
Foundation: Walk-out basement standard; crawl space or slab for an additional fee

See index for more information

Images provided by designer/architect

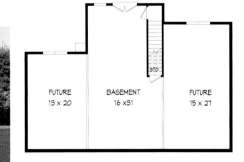

VAULTED REAR PORCH
17 x 8

DECK
14 x 8

DECK
15 x 8

SCREEN PORCH
14 x 6

VAULTED GREAT ROOM
13 x 18

BEDROOM #2
13 x 11

BEDROOM #1
11 x 11

BATH #2
11 x 5

BATH #1
7x10

HALL

VAULTED COUNTRY KITCHEN
16 x 14

BEDROOM #3
13 x 11

UTILITY
4 x 6

SHWR
4 x 6

STACKED W/D

FRONT PORCH
18 x 6

First Floor
1,273 sq. ft.

FUTURE
13 x 20

BASEMENT
16 x31

FUTURE
15 x 27

STO

Optional Lower Level
1,273 sq. ft.

Plan #F12-028D-0100

Dimensions: 46' W x 42'6" D
Heated Sq. Ft.: 1,311
Bedrooms: 3   **Bathrooms:** 2
Exterior Walls: 2" x 6"
Foundation: Crawl space or slab, please specify when ordering

See index for more information

Images provided by designer/architect

© Copyright by designer/architect

Plan #F12-013D-0236

Dimensions: 71'2" W x 64'6" D
Heated Sq. Ft.: 2,183
Bonus Sq. Ft.: 1,670
Bedrooms: 3   **Bathrooms:** 3½
Foundation: Crawl space standard; slab or basement for an additional fee

See index for more information

Images provided by designer/architect

© Copyright by designer/architect

First Floor
2,183 sq. ft.

Optional
Second Floor
1,670 sq. ft.

organizing
Smaller Homes

Your waterfront home may be smaller, but it always seems you still have the same amount of stuff that needs to fit in that home. Just the thought of having to fit all that stuff into a smaller space should not discourage you from trying to stay organized. There are ways to make good use of the space you do have. So sit back and enjoy a room-to-room guide of how to maximize the space in each room of your home.

Make An Entrance

The entryway of a home is the first place your guests will see. No matter the size of the entryway, there is an organized solution for all. First, make sure to scale the furniture to the space so there is plenty of room to open the door as well as room for a comfortable greeting area. For entry halls with a little more space, add a bench that serves as storage as well as a place to put on, or take off shoes. For smaller entry halls, store in style with a chest that has baskets, drawers and doors. Remember mixing your storage is stylish, but still functional.

Get Cozy

Typically the great room generates the most traffic. In order to make the most of this room, make it multipurpose. Add a long couch for during the day seating, and at night it can be used as a guest sleeping area. Have coffee tables or nesting side tables that can be easily moved off to the side to open up floor space, or separated for more table space when entertaining. Consider built-ins for storage so coasters, remotes and other knick-knacks aren't out while entertaining guests. For wall decoration, add mirrors to make the space appear larger.

From Cluttered To Clever

Creating space in the kitchen can often be difficult, and cooking in a cluttered kitchen is even harder. To reduce counter and cabinet clutter, hang pots and cooking utensils from simple towel bars. Another option is hanging the pots and pans above your head. Both options create more cabinet space that can be used for a multitude of other kitchen necessities. The bigger the pantry the better, right? Not necessarily. The more shallow the pantry, the better. You can see everything and nothing gets pushed to the back where it will most likely expire before you use it.

Now that you have the kitchen cabinets more organized, how can you produce more kitchen floor space? Having a table in the middle of the kitchen takes up a large amount of floor space. A kitchen nook can free up kitchen space that would have normally been lost by a free-standing table. The nook provides a cozy eating area and can even have extra storage drawers built-in for even more organization.

Let us move to the second floor of the home. But first, do not let any space go to waste including under the stairs. For steep stairs, there is sufficient room to add a sitting area. If your stairs are not steep, there are a few creative effects to execute that allow for no wasted space. Construct a cozy reading nook with built-in drawers to arrange books and magazines. Another fun thing to do with the space is to build shelves or drawers for any odds and ends that do not have a specific place in your home.

Messy No More

The easiest way to create more space in a bedroom is to choose a tall bed frame. With a taller bed frame, you can use under-the-bed boxes to store things that are not used on a regular basis. Plastic bins are also an inexpensive, easy organization solution for children's toys. Make the most of your closet by moving the hanging rod up and adding another row of hanging space. This will double your hanging capabilities. Consider adding a chest or ottoman at the end of the bed that can be used as pillow and blanket storage.

Tiny Can Be Tidy

The bathroom is not the first room you would think of saving space in. But, there are some space saving tricks to increase bathroom space. Depending on the size of the bathroom, adding tall, vertical free-standing shelves to store toilet paper, towels, and other bathroom necessities can be handy. If the bathroom is small, add shelves above the toilet to help store bathroom necessities in an attractive way.

Mud Stays In The Mud Room

It is easy for the mud room to become cluttered and unorganized because it is the first room families usually enter and set stuff down in. If you have children, get the kids to help with the organization. Create a locker for each child. They can hang coats, backpacks and put their shoes there so they're organized and right by the door. If you do not have enough wall space for lockers, or you do not have kids, hooks are a trendy way to store coats, purses, and all those belongings you need as you are running out the door each day.

Now that you have been guided through each room in the home, you should be able to fit everything in the rooms effortlessly without having to downsize as many belongings. And, another tip to always remember, when shopping for furniture for a smaller home, select furniture that can double as storage space. And, you always want to pick furniture that will maximize your floor space as much as possible, so choose smaller sized pieces that don't take up too much floor space.

Unless noted, all images copyrighted by the designer/architect. Page 126, left, top to bottom: Plan #F12-101D-0155 on page 32; Standard Fusion Shower Pan™, trendingaccessibility.com; Honey-Can-Do International Shelf Space Saver, amazon.com; middle: narrow bookcase, istockphoto.com; right: Teak Bathroom Shelf, signaturehardware.com; Page 127, clockwise, top left: Small mud space minimal style, nextluxury.com; Bucket storage idea, bhg.com; Plan #011S-0189; Built-ins make it easy, nextluxury.com; See more photos and purchase plans at houseplansandmore.com.

Plan #F12-141D-0211

Dimensions: 33'4" W x 49'3" D
Heated Sq. Ft.: 2,310
Bedrooms: 5   **Bathrooms:** 3
Foundation: Pier standard; crawl space, slab, basement or walk-out basement for an additional fee

See index for more information

Images provided by designer/architect

Lower Level

© Copyright by designer/architect

Second Floor
935 sq. ft.

First Floor
1,375 sq. ft.

Plan #F12-139D-0040

Dimensions: 34'6" W x 52'6" D
Heated Sq. Ft.: 2,206
Bedrooms: 4   **Bathrooms:** 3½
Exterior Walls: 2" x 6"
Foundation: Basement standard; crawl space, slab, daylight basement or walk-out basement for an additional fee

See index for more information

Second Floor
1,048 sq. ft.

Images provided by designer/architect

© Copyright by designer/architect

Lower Level

First Floor
1,158 sq. ft.

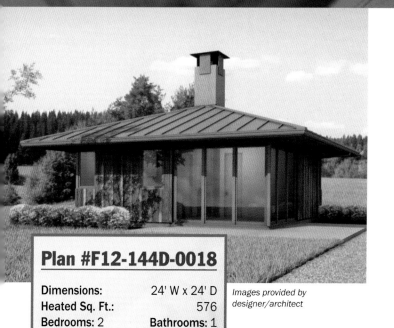

Plan #F12-144D-0018

Dimensions:	24' W x 24' D
Heated Sq. Ft.:	576
Bedrooms: 2	Bathrooms: 1
Exterior Walls:	2" x 6"
Foundation:	Crawl space

See index for more information

Images provided by designer/architect

© Copyright by designer/architect

Plan #F12-011D-0677

Dimensions:	38' W x 72' D
Heated Sq. Ft.:	1,922
Bedrooms: 3	Bathrooms: 2
Exterior Walls:	2" x 6"
Foundation:	Crawl space or slab standard; basement for an additional fee

See index for more information

Images provided by designer/architect

© Copyright by designer/architect

Plan #F12-028D-0093

Dimensions:	34' W x 62'3" D
Heated Sq. Ft.:	1,587
Bedrooms: 3	**Bathrooms:** 2
Exterior Walls:	2" x 6"

Foundation: Crawl space or slab, please specify when ordering

See index for more information

Images provided by designer/architect

Features

- This Craftsman bungalow promises to be a stand-out in any neighborhood with its raised covered front porch and its classic Craftsman shingle siding and column style
- The great room is adorned with a cozy fireplace on one wall and is surrounded by windows
- The kitchen is designed with efficiency in mind, while still offering added amenities like a center island and an eating bar for two
- The rear entrance from the screened porch has a built-in bench with added storage
- The rear covered porch is ideal for a grill, or private relaxation time

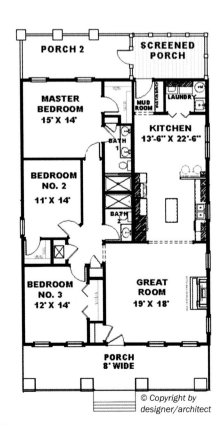

PORCH 2

SCREENED PORCH

MASTER BEDROOM
15' X 14'

MUD ROOM

LAUNDRY

KITCHEN
13'-6" X 22'-6"

BATH

BEDROOM NO. 2
11' X 14'

BATH

BEDROOM NO. 3
12' X 14'

GREAT ROOM
19' X 18'

PORCH 8' WIDE

© Copyright by designer/architect

houseplansandmore.com

Plan #F12-123D-0211

Dimensions:	70' W x 88' D
Heated Sq. Ft.:	1,954
Bonus Sq. Ft.:	1,030
Bedrooms: 2	**Bathrooms:** 2½

Foundation: Walk-out basement standard; crawl space, slab or basement for an additional fee

See index for more information

Features

- A wonderful home for a hillside or sloping waterfront lot
- Enter the great room and find an open floor plan with the kitchen and island overlooking the great room with a dining area nearby
- There's a lovely screened deck, perfect for alfresco dining with a view and right next to a huge covered deck running the length of the back of the home ideal when the grill is fired up
- An en-suite guest bedroom will ensure your family and friends will never want to leave
- The optional lower level has an additional 1,030 square feet of living area with a family room with fireplace and wet bar, a game table area, a laundry room, two bedrooms, and a full bath
- 2-car side entry garage

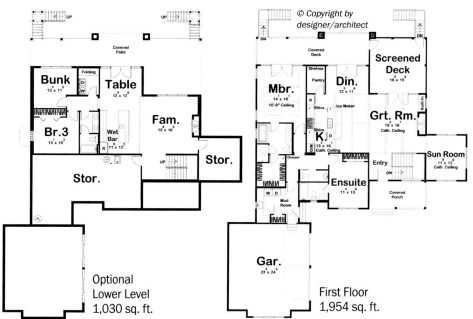

Images provided by designer/architect

Optional Lower Level 1,030 sq. ft.

First Floor 1,954 sq. ft.

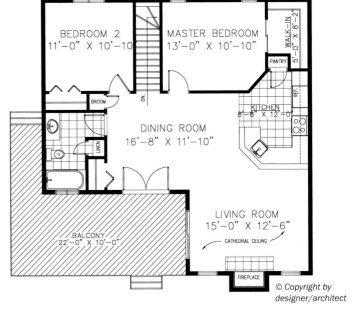

Plan #F12-148D-0205

Dimensions:	34' W x 34' D
Heated Sq. Ft.:	987
Bedrooms: 2	Bathrooms: 1
Exterior Walls:	2" x 6"
Foundation:	Basement

See index for more information

Images provided by designer/architect

© Copyright by designer/architect

BEDROOM 2
11'-0" X 10'-10"

MASTER BEDROOM
13'-0" X 10'-10"

WALK-IN
5'-0" X 8'-2"

PANTRY

BROOM

DN

REF.

KITCHEN
8'-8" X 12'-0"

LINEN

DINING ROOM
16'-8" X 11'-10"

LIVING ROOM
15'-0" X 12'-6"

CATHEDRAL CEILING

BALCONY
22'-0" X 10'-0"

FIREPLACE

Plan #F12-007D-0085

Dimensions:	59'8" W x 40' D
Heated Sq. Ft.:	1,787
Bonus Sq. Ft.:	415
Bedrooms: 3	Bathrooms: 2
Foundation:	Walk-out basement

See index for more information

Images provided by designer/architect

Deck

Garage Below

skylights above

Great Rm
23-8x15-4
vaulted

plant shelf above

MBr
15-6x14-6
vaulted

Brk'ft

P

Hall

W D

Laun.

Kitchen
14-7x15-8

Dining
11-1x13-8

Entry

Dn

L

R

DW

Porch

Br 3
12-0x12-0

Br 2
12-0x12-0

Shelves

vaulted

First Floor
1,787 sq. ft.

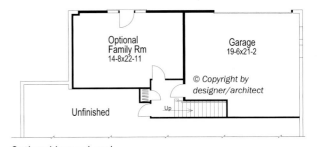

Optional
Family Rm
14-8x22-11

Garage
19-6x21-2

© Copyright by designer/architect

Unfinished

Up

Optional Lower Level
415 sq. ft.

Plan #F12-058D-0244

Dimensions:	28'8" W x 34'10" D
Heated Sq. Ft.:	747
Bedrooms: 1	Bathrooms: 1
Foundation:	Slab

See index for more information

Images provided by designer/architect

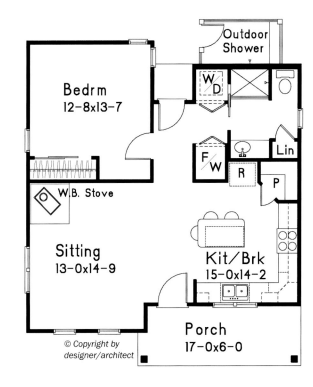

Outdoor Shower

Bedrm
12-8x13-7

W/D

F/W R Lin P

W.B. Stove

Sitting
13-0x14-9

Kit/Brk
15-0x14-2

Porch
17-0x6-0

© Copyright by designer/architect

Plan #F12-007D-0124

Dimensions:	65' W x 51' D
Heated Sq. Ft.:	1,944
Bedrooms: 3	Bathrooms: 2
Foundation:	Basement standard; crawl space or slab for an additional fee

See index for more information

Images provided by designer/architect

Detached Garage
34-4x23-4

Patio

Brk fst /
Hearth Rm
12-0x16-0

Patio

Laun.

Covered Patio

MBr
16-10x13-7
Coffered clg.

Kitchen
12-0x
10-3

Great Rm
19-10x24-8
Vaulted

Hall

Br 2
11-2x12-0

Br 3
10-1x12-0

Entry

© Copyright by designer/architect   Porch

Home Plans Index

Plan Number	Square Feet	PDF File	5-Sets	CAD File	Material List	Page	Plan Number	Square Feet	PDF File	5-Sets	CAD File	Material List	Page
F12-001D-0031	1,501	$1,049	$1,049	$1,649	$125	121	F12-024D-0813	1,728	$1,728	-	$1,878	-	26
F12-001D-0041	1,000	$849	$849	$1,249	$125	66	F12-024D-0819	2,530	$2,530	-	$2,530	-	64
F12-001D-0067	1,285	$949	$949	$1,449	$125	72	F12-024S-0021	5,862	$3,025	-	$3,025	-	111
F12-001D-0085	720	$649	$649	$1,049	$125	105	F12-026D-2011	1,750	$1,055	-	$1,740	$175	25
F12-001D-0086	1,154	$949	$949	$1,449	$125	62	F12-026D-2035	2,597	$1,155	-	$1,920	-	117
F12-007D-0039	1,530	$1,049	$1,049	-	$125	120	F12-028D-0060	1,640	$920	$1,020	-	-	95
F12-007D-0055	2,029	$1,149	$1,149	$1,849	$125	71	F12-028D-0064	1,292	$795	$910	-	-	17
F12-007D-0068	1,922	$1,049	$1,049	$1,649	$125	114	F12-028D-0090	992	$745	$810	-	$100	42
F12-007D-0085	1,787	$1,049	$1,049	$1,649	$125	132	F12-028D-0093	1,587	$920	$1,020	-	-	130
F12-007D-0105	1,084	$849	$849	$1,249	$125	62	F12-028D-0100	1,311	$795	$910	-	$100	123
F12-007D-0124	1,944	$1,049	$1,049	$1,649	$125	133	F12-028D-0103	1,520	$920	$1,020	-	-	54
F12-007D-0140	1,591	$1,049	$1,049	$1,649	$125	82	F12-028D-0109	890	$745	$810	-	-	47
F12-007D-0244	1,605	$1,049	$1,049	$1,649	$125	46	F12-032D-0032	1,574	$1,190	$1,315	$1,790	-	31
F12-008D-0133	624	$649	$649	-	$125	109	F12-032D-0036	1,285	$1,110	$1,235	$1,710	-	16
F12-008D-0153	792	$649	$649	$1,049	$125	71	F12-032D-0357	874	$915	$1,040	$1,515	-	67
F12-008D-0161	618	$649	$649		$125	68	F12-032D-0368	1,625	$1,190	$1,315	$1,790	-	61
F12-008D-0162	865	$849	$849	-	$125	99	F12-032D-0553	1,297	$1,110	$1,235	$1,710	-	18
F12-011D-0037	2,262	$1,578	$1,778	$3,156	$275	18	F12-032D-0708	400	$890	$1,015	$1,490	-	36
F12-011D-0307	1,529	$1,201	$1,401	$2,402	$275	116	F12-032D-0709	480	$890	$1,015	$1,490	-	119
F12-011D-0335	2,557	$1,540	$1,740	$3,080	$275	22	F12-032D-0861	1,301	$1,110	$1,235	$1,710	-	20
F12-011D-0617	2,104	$1,495	$1,695	$2,990	$275	73	F12-032D-0872	629	$890	$1,015	$1,490	-	94
F12-011D-0627	1,878	$1,331	$1,531	$2,662	$275	81	F12-032D-0874	576	$890	$1,015	$1,490	-	63
F12-011D-0630	2,495	$1,525	$1,725	$3,050	$275	122	F12-032D-0935	1,050	$1,020	$1,145	$1,620	-	82
F12-011D-0637	1,744	$1,292	$1,492	$2,584	$275	72	F12-032D-1076	2,146	$1,255	$1,380	$1,855	-	117
F12-011D-0642	2,608	$1,523	$1,723	$3,046	$275	29	F12-032D-1110	1,704	$1,190	$1,315	$1,790	-	33
F12-011D-0655	2,707	$1,672	$1,872	$3,344	$275	67	F12-032D-1134	2,652	$1,390	$1,515	$1,990	-	80
F12-011D-0660	1,704	$1,288	$1,488	$2,576	$275	95	F12-032D-1142	1,209	$1,110	$1,235	$1,710	-	14
F12-011D-0677	1,922	$1,296	$1,496	$2,592	$275	129	F12-048D-0008	2,089	$1,050	$1,250	$2,100	-	66
F12-011D-0679	1,821	$1,294	$1,494	$2,588	$275	77	F12-051D-0970	1,354	$1,107	$882	$1,744	-	106
F12-011D-0683	944	$958	$1,158	$1,916	$275	121	F12-055D-0317	2,611	$1,100	$1,200	$2,200	-	21
F12-013D-0133	953	$945	$995	$1,350	$195	48	F12-056D-0096	2,510	$2,295	-	$3,245	-	57
F12-013D-0181	1,975	$1,195	$1,245	$1,695	$195	42	F12-056D-0098	3,123	$2,195	-	$3,245	-	52
F12-013D-0216	1,488	$1,045	$1,145	$1,495	$195	79	F12-056D-0120	1,729	$1,795	-	$2,645	-	21
F12-013D-0218	1,500	$1,195	$1,245	$1,695	-	54	F12-056D-0134	4,917	$2,495	-	$3,545	-	25
F12-013D-0231	1,604	$1,195	$1,245	$1,695	-	43	F12-056D-0141	2,510	$1,998	-	$2,948	-	41
F12-013D-0236	2,183	$1,295	$1,345	$1,795	$195	123	F12-058D-0010	676	$550	-	$650	$80	47
F12-013D-0240	2,799	$1,295	$1,345	$1,795	$195	60	F12-058D-0196	867	$550	-	$650	$80	68
F12-013D-0243	514	$945	$995	$1,350	$195	35	F12-058D-0197	781	$550	-	$650	$80	103
F12-017D-0010	1,660	$940	$1,050	$1,135	$95	65	F12-058D-0199	1,158	$550	-	$650	$80	69
F12-019D-0048	2,248	$1,895	-	$2,995	-	102	F12-058D-0201	1,191	$550	-	$650	$80	37
F12-020D-0250	2,020	$1,100	$1,230	$2,100	$90	24	F12-058D-0202	740	$550	-	$650	$80	29
F12-020D-0397	1,608	$1,000	$1,130	$1,900	-	103	F12-058D-0204	1,185	$550	-	$650	$80	105
F12-024D-0008	1,650	$1,540	$920	$1,775	-	45	F12-058D-0205	1,179	$550	-	$650	$80	116
F12-024D-0013	1,863	$1,190	$890	-	-	16	F12-058D-0238	1,149	$625	-	$725	$80	113
F12-024D-0312	1,936	$1,190	$890	$1,695	-	24	F12-058D-0243	1,268	$550	-	$650	$80	96

Home Plans Index

Plan Number	Square Feet	PDF File	5-Sets	CAD File	Material List	Page	Plan Number	Square Feet	PDF File	5-Sets	CAD File	Material List	Page
F12-058D-0244	747	$550	-	$650	$80	133	F12-126D-1029	1,036	$875	$716	$1,463	$105	94
F12-062D-0047	1,230	$700	$800	$1,400	$85	49	F12-126D-1151	1,060	$875	$716	$1,463	$105	35
F12-069D-0106	736	$649	$649		$125	37	F12-126D-1175	910	$875	$716	$1,463	$105	34
F12-076D-0220	3,061	$1,950	$1,200	$2,600	-	38	F12-126D-1342	1,108	$1,007	$769	$1,564	$115	115
F12-077D-0019	1,400	$1,300	$1,200	$1,725	$150	83	F12-128D-0060	2,309	$1,100	$800		-	17
F12-077D-0297	904	$1,175	$1,075	$1,575	$125	115	F12-128D-0318	1,966	$1,000	$700		-	92
F12-080D-0001	583	$695	$575		$95	20	F12-139D-0005	2,180	$1,495	$1,620	$2,995	-	34
F12-080D-0004	1,154	$895	$675		$95	19	F12-139D-0040	2,206	$1,495	$1,620	$2,995	-	128
F12-080D-0012	1,370	$895	$675		$95	53	F12-141D-0012	1,972	$1,533	$1,764	$2,303	$295	91
F12-082D-0065	1,783	$2,083	$1,783		-	118	F12-141D-0021	1,267	$1,323	$1,554	$2,023	-	98
F12-082S-0001	6,816	$5,500	$5,000	$6,000	-	74	F12-141D-0025	2,033	$1,673	$1,904	$2,443	$295	107
F12-084D-0090	2,221	$1,195	$1,290	$2,145	-	113	F12-141D-0026	1,500	$1,393	$1,624	$2,093	$295	77
F12-088D-0242	2,281	$1,430	$1,320	$1,430	-	73	F12-141D-0051	2,000	$1,533	$1,764	$2,303	-	30
F12-091D-0506	2,241	$2,050	$2,250	$2,700	$450	40	F12-141D-0061	1,273	$1,323	$1,554	$2,023	$295	44
F12-101D-0056	2,593	$1,650	-	$2,950	-	90	F12-141D-0084	1,841	$1,533	$1,764	$2,303	-	28
F12-101D-0057	2,037	$1,450	-	$2,750	-	84	F12-141D-0211	2,310	$1,813	$2,044	$2,583	-	128
F12-101D-0115	2,251	$1,450	-	$2,750	-	58	F12-141D-0220	1,361	$1,323	$1,554	$2,023	-	112
F12-101D-0119	3,063	$1,850	-	$3,350	-	19	F12-141D-0233	1,835	$1,533	$1,764	$2,303	-	108
F12-101D-0124	3,338	$2,100	-	$3,600	-	12	F12-141D-0252	2,016	$1,673	$1,904	$2,443	-	79
F12-101D-0125	2,970	$1,850	-	$3,350	-	50	F12-141D-0282	1,359	$1,323	$1,554	$2,023	$295	93
F12-101D-0142	2,700	$1,650	-	$2,950	-	28	F12-141D-0323	1,787	$1,533	$1,764	$2,303	-	85
F12-101D-0147	2,538	$1,650	-	$2,950	-	55	F12-141D-0346	1,412	$1,323	$1,554	$2,023	-	76
F12-101D-0155	952	$1,350	-	$2,650	-	32	F12-141D-0442	1,727	$1,323	$1,554	$2,023	-	69
F12-111D-0032	1,094	$995	-	$1,995	-	23	F12-141D-0456	1,273	$1,953	$2,184	$2,723	-	122
F12-111D-0051	2,346	$1,445	-	$2,445	-	30	F12-141D-0460	2,650	$1,953	$2,184	$2,723	-	46
F12-111D-0074	2,005	$1,445	-	$2,445	-	83	F12-141D-0461	2,061	$1,673	$1,904	$2,443	-	99
F12-121D-0016	1,582	$1,049	$1,049	$1,649	$125	48	F12-141D-0466	3,288	$2,793	$3,024	$3,563	-	22
F12-121D-0023	1,762	$1,049	$1,049	$1,649	$125	120	F12-141D-0479	1,740	$1,393	$1,624	$1,685	-	104
F12-121D-0025	1,368	$949	$949	$1,449	$125	63	F12-142D-7584	793	$1,113	$1,344	$1,533	-	96
F12-122D-0001	1,105	$949	$949	$1,449	$125	102	F12-144D-0001	1,677	$1,150	$1,275	$1,645	$95	55
F12-123D-0202	1,856	$1,300	-	$1,800	$150	15	F12-144D-0017	1,043	$1,090	$1,215	$1,585	-	78
F12-123D-0211	1,954	$1,300	-	$1,800	$150	131	F12-144D-0018	576	$1,040	$1,165	$1,535	-	129
F12-123D-0258	1,695	$1,200	-	$1,700	$150	70	F12-144D-0024	1,024	$1,090	$1,215	$1,585	$95	104
F12-123D-0263	756	$800	-	$1,300	$150	56	F12-148D-0008	1,072	$1,273	$892	$1,897	-	36
F12-123D-0264	733	$800	-	$1,300	$150	93	F12-148D-0047	720	$1,273	$892	$1,897	-	92
F12-126D-0197	772	$742	$567	$1,378	$95	97	F12-148D-0048	1,217	$1,273	$892	$1,897	-	31
F12-126D-0993	572	$742	$567	$1,378	$95	78	F12-148D-0205	987	$1,273	$892	$1,897	-	132
F12-126D-1001	1,104	$1,007	$769	$1,564	$115	49	F12-155D-0100	970	$1,100	$1,200	$2,200	-	114
F12-126D-1003	624	$742	$567	$1,378	$95	108	F12-155D-0220	696	$700	$800	$1,400	-	70
F12-126D-1005	1,133	$1,007	$769	$1,564	$115	43	F12-156D-0014	551	$675	$775	$1,475	-	97
F12-126D-1012	815	$742	$567	$1,378	$95	112	F12-161D-0001	4,036	$2,095	$2,295	$2,895	-	100
F12-126D-1016	756	$742	$567	$1,378	$95	98	F12-163D-0003	1,416	$1,450	-	$1,825	-	110
F12-126D-1018	900	$742	$567	$1,378	$95	76	F12-163D-0013	1,676	$1,850	-	$2,075	-	109
F12-126D-1019	924	$875	$716	$1,463	$105	64	F12-170D-0003	2,672	$945	$995	$1,795	-	23
F12-126D-1022	1,156	$1,007	$769	$1,564	$115	65							

why buy
STOCK PLANS?

Building a home yourself presents many opportunities to showcase your creativity, individuality, and dreams turned into reality. With these opportunities, many challenges and questions will crop up. Location, size, and budget are all important to consider, as well as special features and amenities. When you begin to examine everything, it can become overwhelming to search for your dream home. But, before you get too anxious, start the search process an easier way and choose a home design that's a stock home plan.

Custom home plans, as well as stock home plans, offer positives and negatives; what is "best" can only be determined by your lifestyle, budget, and time. A customized home plan is one that a homeowner and designer or architect work together to develop from scratch, taking ideas and putting them down on paper. These plans require extra patience, as it may be months before the architect has them drawn and ready. A stock plan is a pre-developed plan that fits the needs and desires of a group of people, or the general population. These are often available within days of purchasing and typically cost up to one-tenth of the price of customized home plans. They still have all of the amenities you were looking for in a home, and usually at a much more affordable price than having custom plans drawn for you.

When compared to a customized plan, some homeowners fear that a stock home will be a carbon copy home, taking away the opportunity for individualism and creating a unique design. This is a common misconception that can waste a lot of money and time!

As you can see from the home designs throughout this book, the variety of stock plans available is truly impressive, encompassing the most up-to-date features and amenities. With a little patience, browse the numerous available stock plans available throughout this book, and easily purchase a plan and be ready to build almost immediately.

Plus, stock plans can be customized. For example, perhaps you see a stock plan that is just about perfect, but you wish the mud room was a tad larger. Rather than go through the cost and time of having a custom home design drawn, you could have our customizing service modify the stock home plan and have your new dream plan ready to go in no time. Also, stock home plans often have a material list available, helping to eliminate unknown costs from developing during construction.

It's often a good idea to speak with someone who has recently built. Did they use stock or custom plans? What would they recommend you do, or do not undertake? Can they recommend professionals that will help you narrow down your options? As you take a look at plans throughout this publication, don't hesitate to take notes, or write down questions. Also, take advantage of our website, houseplansandmore.com. This website is very user-friendly, allowing you to search for the perfect house design by style, size, budget, and a home's features. With all of these tools readily available to you, you'll find the home design of your dreams in no time at all, thanks to the innovative stock plans readily available today that take into account your wishes in a floor plan as well as your wallet.

how can I find out if I can AFFORD to build a home?

The most important question for someone wanting to build a new home is, "How much is it going to cost?" Obviously, you must have an accurate budget set before ordering house plans and beginning construction, or your dream home will quickly turn into a nightmare. We make building your dream home a much simpler reality thanks to the estimated cost-to-build report available for all of the home plans in this book and on our website, houseplansandmore.com. Price is always the number one factor when choosing a new home. Price dictates the size and the quality of materials you will use. So, it comes as no surprise that having an accurate building estimate prior to making your final decision on a home plan quite possibly is the most important step. If you feel you've found "the" home, then before buying the plans, order a cost-to-build report for the zip code where you want to build. This report is created specifically for you when ordered, and it will educate you on all costs associated with building the home. Simply order the cost-to-build report on houseplansandmore.com for the home design you want to build and gain knowledge of the material and labor cost. Not only does the report allow you to choose the quality of the materials, you can also select from various options from lot condition to contractor fees. Successfully manage your construction budget in all areas, clearly see where the majority of the costs lie, and save money from start to finish. Listed to the right are the categories included in a cost-to-build report. Each category breaks down labor cost, material cost, funds needed, and the report offers the ability to manipulate over/under adjustments if necessary.

Budget includes your contact information, the state and zip code where you intend to build and material class. This section also includes: square footage, number of windows, fireplaces, balconies, baths, garage location and size, decks, foundation type, and bonus room square footage.

General Soft Costs include cost for plans, customizing (if applicable), building permits, pre-construction services, and planning expenses.

Site Work & Utilities include water, sewer, electric, and gas. Choose the type of site work and if you'll need a driveway.

Foundation includes a menu that lists the most common types.

Framing Rough Shell calculates rough framing costs including framing for fireplaces, balconies, decks, porches, basements and bonus rooms.

Roofing includes several common options.

Dry Out Shell allows you to select doors, windows, and siding.

Electrical includes wiring and the quality of the light fixtures.

Plumbing includes labor costs, plumbing materials, plumbing fixtures, and fire proofing materials.

HVAC includes costs for both labor and materials.

Insulation includes costs for both labor and materials.

Finish Shell includes drywall, interior doors and trim, stairs, shower doors, mirrors, bath accessories, and labor costs.

Cabinets & Vanities select the grade of your cabinets, vanities, kitchen countertops, and bathroom vanity materials, as well as appliances.

Painting includes all painting materials, paint quality, and labor.

Flooring includes over a dozen flooring material options.

Special Equipment Needs calculate cost for unforeseen expenses.

Contractor Fee / Project Manager includes the cost of your cost-to-build report, project manager and/or general contractor fees. If you're doing the managing yourself, your costs will be tremendously lower in this section.

Land Payoff includes the cost of your land.

Reserves / Closing Costs includes interest, contingency reserves, and closing costs.

We've taken the guesswork out of figuring out what your new home is going to cost. Take control of construction, determine the major expenses, and save money. Supervise all costs, from labor to materials and manage construction with confidence, which allows you to avoid costly mistakes and unforeseen expenses. To order a Cost-To-Build Report, visit houseplansandmore.com and search for the specific plan. Then, look for the button that says, "Request Your Report" and get started.

what kind of
PLAN PACKAGE do I need?

Please Note: *Not all plan packages listed below are available for every plan. There may be additional plan options available. Please visit houseplansandmore.com for all of a plan's options and pricing, or call 1-800-373-2646 for all current options. The plan pricing shown in this book is subject to change without notice.*

5-Set Plan Package

includes five complete sets of construction drawings. Besides one set for yourself, additional sets of blueprints will be required for your lender, your local building department, your contractor, and any other tradespeople working on your project. Please note: These 5 sets of plans are copyrighted, so they can't be altered or copied.

8-Set Plan Package

includes eight complete sets of construction drawings. Besides one set for yourself, additional sets of blueprints will be required for your lender, your local building department, your contractor, and any other tradespeople working on your project. Please note: These 8 sets of plans are copyrighted, so they can't be altered or copied.

Reproducible Masters

is one complete paper set of construction drawings that can be modified. They include a one-time build copyright release that allows you to draw changes on the plans. This allows you, your builder, or local design professional to make the necessary drawing changes without the major expense of entirely redrawing the plans. Easily make minor drawing changes by using correction fluid to cover up small areas of the existing drawing, then draw in your modifications. Once the plan has been altered to fit your needs, you have the right to copy, or reproduce the modified plans as needed for building your home. Please note: The right of building only one home from these plans is licensed exclusively to the buyer. You may not use this design to build a second or multiple dwelling(s) without purchasing a multi-build license (see page 143 for more information).

PDF File Format

is our most popular plan package option because of how fast you can receive them your blueprints (usually within 24 to 48 hours Monday through Friday), and their ability to be easily shared via email with your contractor, subcontractors, and local building officials. The PDF file format is a complete set of construction drawings in an electronic file format. It includes a one-time build copyright release that allows you to make changes and copies of the plans. Typically you will receive a PDF file via email within 24-48 hours (Mon-Fri, 7:30am-4:30pm CST) allowing you to save money on shipping. Upon receiving, visit a local copy or print shop and print the number of plans you need to build your home, or print one and alter the plan by using correction fluid and drawing in your modifications. Please note: These are flat image files and cannot be altered electronically. PDF files are non-refundable and not returnable.

CAD File Format

is the actual computer files for a plan directly from AutoCAD, or another computer aided design program. CAD files are the best option if you have a significant amount of changes to make to the plan, or if you need to make the plan fit your local codes. If you purchase a CAD File, it allows you, or a local design professional the ability to modify the plans electronically in a CAD program, so making changes to the plan is easier and less expensive than using a paper set of plans when modifying. A CAD package also includes a one-time build copyright release that allows you to legally make your changes, and print multiple copies of the plan. See the index for availability and pricing. Please note: CAD files are non-refundable and not returnable.

Mirror Reverse Sets

Sometimes a home fits a site better if it is flipped left to right. A mirror reverse set of plans is simply a mirror image of the original drawings causing the lettering and dimensions to read backwards. Therefore, when ordering a mirror reverse set of plans, you must purchase at least one set of the original plans to read from, and use the mirror reverse set for construction. Some plans offer right reading reverse for an additional fee. This means the plan has been redrawn by the designer as the mirrored version and can easily be read.

Additional Sets

You can order extra plan sets of a plan for an additional fee. A 5-set, 8-set, or reproducible master must have been previously purchased. Please note: Only available within 90 days after purchase of a plan package.

2" x 6" Exterior Walls

can be purchased for some plans for an additional fee (see houseplansandmore.com for availability and pricing).

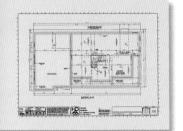

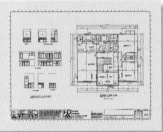

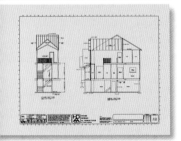

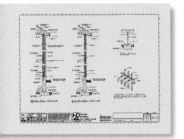

our
PLAN PACKAGES include...

Quality plans for building your future, with extras that provide unsurpassed value, ensure good construction and long-term enjoyment. A quality home - one that looks good, functions well, and provides years of enjoyment - is a product of many things - design, materials, and craftsmanship. But it's also the result of outstanding blueprints - the actual plans and specifications that tell the builder exactly how to build your home.

And with our BLUEPRINT PACKAGES you get the absolute best. A complete set of blueprints is available for every design in this book. These "working drawings" are highly detailed, resulting in two key benefits:

- **BETTER UNDERSTANDING BY THE CONTRACTOR OF HOW TO BUILD YOUR HOME AND...**
- **MORE ACCURATE CONSTRUCTION ESTIMATES THAT WILL SAVE YOU TIME AND MONEY.**

Below is a sample of the plan information included for most of the designs in this book. Specific details may vary with each designer's plan. While this information is typical for most plans, we cannot assure the inclusion of all the following referenced items. Please contact us at 1-800-373-2646 for a plan's specific information, including which of the following items are included.

1 cover sheet is included with many of the plans, the cover sheet is the artist's rendering of the exterior of the home. It will give you an idea of how your home will look when completed and landscaped.

2 foundation plan shows the layout of the basement, walk-out basement, crawl space, slab or pier foundation. All necessary notations and dimensions are included. See plan page for the foundation types included. If the home plan you choose does not have your desired foundation type, our Customer Service Representatives can advise you on how to customize your foundation to suit your specific needs or site conditions.

3 floor plans show the placement of walls, doors, closets, plumbing fixtures, electrical outlets, columns, and beams for each level of the home.

4 interior elevations provide views of special interior elements such as fireplaces, kitchen cabinets, built-in units and other features of the home.

5 exterior elevations illustrate the front, rear and both sides of the house, with all details of exterior materials and the required dimensions.

6 sections show detail views of the home or portions of the home as if it were sliced from the roof to the foundation. This sheet shows important areas such as load-bearing walls, stairs, joists, trusses and other structural elements, which are critical for proper construction.

7 details show how to construct certain components of your home, such as the roof system, stairs, deck, etc.

do you want to make
CHANGES to your plan?

We understand that sometimes it is difficult to find blueprints that meet all of your specific needs.
That is why we offer home plan modification services so you can build a home exactly the way you want it!

Are You Thinking About Customizing A Plan?

If you're like many customers, you may want to make changes to your home plan to make it the dream home you've always wanted. That's where our expert design and modification partners come in. You won't find a more efficient and economic way to get your changes done than by using our home plan customizing services.

Whether it's enlarging a kitchen, adding a porch, or converting a crawl space to a basement, we can customize any plan and make it perfect for your needs. Simply create your wish list and let us go to work. Soon you'll have the blueprints for your new home, and at a fraction of the cost of hiring a local architect!

It's Easy!
- We can customize any of the plans in this book, or on houseplansandmore.com.
- We provide a FREE cost estimate for your home plan modifications within 24-48 hours (Monday-Friday, 7:30am-4:30pm CST).
- Average turn-around time to complete the modifications is typically 4-5 weeks.
- You will receive one-on-one design consultations.

Customizing Facts
- The average cost to have a house plan customized is typically less than 1 percent of the building costs — compare that to the national average of 7 percent of building costs.
- The average modification cost for a home is typically $800 to $1,500. This does not include the cost of purchasing the PDF file format of the blueprints, which is required to legally make plan changes.

Other Helpful Information
- Sketch, or make a specific list of changes you'd like to make on the Home Plan Modification Request Form.
- A home plan modification specialist will contact you within 24-48 hours with your free estimate.
- Upon accepting the estimate, you will need to purchase the PDF or CAD file format.
- A contract, which includes a specific list of changes and fees will be sent to you prior for your approval.
- Upon approving the contract, our design partners will keep you up to date by emailing sketches throughout the project.
- Plans can be converted to metric, or to a Barrier-free layout (also referred to as a universal home design, which allows easy mobility for an individual with limitations of any kind).

2 easy steps

1 visit
houseplansandmore.com and click on the Resources tab at the top of the home page, then click "How to Customize Your House Plan," or scan the QR code here to download the Home Plan Modification Request Form.

2 email
your completed form to: customizehpm@designamerica.com, or fax it to: 651-602-5050.

If you are not able to access the Internet, please call 1-800-373-2646 (Monday - Friday, 7:30am - 4:30 pm CST).

helpful BUILDING AIDS

Your Blueprint Package will contain all of the necessary construction information you need to build your home. But, we also offer the following products and services to save you time and money during the building process.

Material List
Many of the home plans in this book have a material list available for purchase that gives you the quantity, dimensions, and description of the building materials needed to construct the home (see the index for availability and pricing). Keep in mind, due to variations in local building code requirements, exact material quantities cannot be guaranteed. Note: Material lists are created with the standard foundation type only. Please review the material list and the construction drawings with your material supplier to verify measurements and quantities of the materials listed before ordering supplies.

The Legal Kit
Avoid many legal pitfalls and build your home with confidence using the forms and contracts featured in this kit. Included are request for proposal documents, various fixed price and cost plus contracts, instructions on how and when to use each form, warranty statements and more. Save time and money before you break ground on your new home or start a remodeling project. All forms are reproducible. This kit is ideal for homebuilders and contractors. Cost: $35

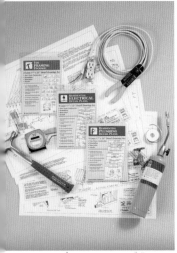

Detail Plan Packages - Plumbing, Framing & Electrical
Three separate packages offer homebuilders details for constructing various foundations; numerous floor, wall and roof framing techniques; simple to complex residential wiring; sump and water softener hookups; plumbing connection methods; installation of septic systems, and more. Each package includes three dimensional illustrations and a glossary of terms. Purchase one or all three. Please note: These drawings do not pertain to a specific home plan, but they include general guidelines and tips for construction in all 3 of these trades. Cost: $30 each or all three for $60

Express Delivery
Most orders are processed within 24 hours of receipt. Please allow 7-10 business days for standard delivery. If you need to place a rush order, please call us by 11:00 am Monday through Friday CST and ask for express service (allow 1-2 business days). Please see page 143 for all shipping and handling charges.

Technical Assistance
If you have questions about your blueprints, we offer technical assistance by calling 1-314-770-2228 between 7:30 am and 4:30 pm Monday through Friday CST. Whether it involves design modifications or field assistance, our home plans team is extremely familiar with all of our home designs and will be happy to help. We want your home to be everything you expect it to be.

before you ORDER

Please note: Plan pricing is subject to change without notice. For current pricing, visit houseplansandmore.com, or call us at 1-800-373-2646.

Building Code Requirements
At the time the construction drawings were prepared, every effort was made to ensure that these plans and specifications met nationally recognized codes. These plans conform to most national building codes. Because building codes vary from area to area, some drawing modifications and/or the assistance of a professional designer or architect may be necessary to comply with your local codes, or to accommodate your specific building site conditions. We advise you to consult with your local building official, or a local builder for information regarding codes governing your area prior to ordering blueprints.

Copyright
Plans are protected under Copyright Law. Reproduction by any means is strictly prohibited. The right of building only one structure from all plan packages is licensed exclusively to the buyer and the plans may not be resold unless by express written authorization from the home designer, or architect. You may not use this plan to build a second or multiple structure(s) without purchasing a multi-build license. Each violation of the Copyright Law is punishable in a fine.

License To Build
When you purchase a "full set of construction drawings" from Design America, Inc., you are purchasing an exclusive one-time "License to Build," not the rights to the design. Design America, Inc. is granting you permission on behalf of the plan's designer or architect to use the construction drawings one-time for the building of the home. The construction drawings (also referred to as blueprints/ plans and any derivative of that plan whether extensive or minor) are still owned and protected under copyright laws by the original designer. The blueprints/plans cannot be resold, transferred, rented, loaned or used by anyone other than the original purchaser of the "License to Build" without written consent from Design America, Inc., or the plan designer. If you are interested in building the plan more than once, please call 1-800-373-2646 and inquire about purchasing a Multi-Build License that will allow you to build a home design more than one time. Please note: A multi-build license can only be purchased if a CAD file or PDF file were initially purchased.

SHIPPING & HANDLING CHARGES

U.S. SHIPPING -
(AK and HI express only)

Regular (allow 7-10 business days)	$35.00
Priority (allow 3-5 business days)	$55.00
Express* (allow 1-2 business days)	$75.00

CANADA SHIPPING**

Regular (allow 8-12 business days)	$50.00
Express* (allow 3-5 business days)	$100.00

OVERSEAS SHIPPING/INTERNATIONAL
Call, fax, or e-mail (customerservice@designamerica.com) for shipping costs.

* For express delivery please call us by 11:00 am Monday-Friday CST

** Orders may be subject to custom's fees and or duties/taxes.

Note: Shipping and handling does not apply on PDF and CAD File orders. PDF and CAD File orders will be emailed within 24-48 hours (Monday - Friday, 7:30 am - 4:30 pm CST) of purchase.

Exchange Policy
Since blueprints are printed in response to your order, we cannot honor requests for refunds.

Order Form

Please send me the following:

Plan Number: F12-_____

Select Foundation Type: (Select ONE- see plan page for available options).

❏ Slab   ❏ Crawl space   ❏ Basement

❏ Walk-out basement   ❏ Pier

❏ Optional Foundation for an additional fee

   Enter foundation cost here $ _____

Plan Package   Cost

❏ CAD File $ _____

❏ PDF File Format (recommended) $ _____

❏ Reproducible Masters $ _____

❏ 8-Set Plan Package $ _____

❏ 5-Set Plan Package $ _____

See the index on pages 134-135 for the most commonly ordered plan packages, or visit houseplansandmore.com to see current pricing and all plan package options available.

Important Extras

For pricing and Material List availability, see the index on pages 134-135. For the other plan options listed below, visit houseplansandmore.com, or call 1-800-373-2646.

❏ Additional plan sets*:

   _____ set(s) at $_____ per set $ _____

❏ Print in right-reading reverse:

   one-time additional fee of $_____ $ _____

❏ Print in mirror reverse:

   _____ set(s) at $_____ per set $ _____
   (where right reading reverse is not available)

❏ Material list (see the index on pages 134-135) $ _____

❏ Legal Kit (001D-9991, see page 142) $ _____

Detail Plan Packages: (see page 142)

   ❏ Framing   ❏ Electrical   ❏ Plumbing $ _____
   (001D-9992)   (001D-9993)   (001D-9994)

Shipping (see page 143) $ _____

SUBTOTAL $ _____

Sales Tax (MO residents only, add 8.24%) $ _____

TOTAL $ _____

*Available only within 90 days after purchase of plan.

Helpful Tips

- You can upgrade to a different plan package within 90 days of your plan purchase.
- Additional sets cannot be ordered without purchasing 5-Sets, 8-Sets, or Reproducible Masters.

Name _____
                    (Please print or type)

Street _____
                 (Please do not use a P.O. Box)

City _____ State _____

Country _____ Zip _____

Daytime telephone   (_____) _____

E-Mail _____
              (For invoice and tracking information)

Payment   ❏ Bank check/money order. No personal checks.
          Make checks payable to Design America, Inc.

❏ MasterCard   ❏ VISA   ❏ DISCOVER   ❏ American Express Cards

Credit card number _____

Expiration date (mm/yy) _____ CID _____

Signature _____

❏ I hereby authorize Design America, Inc. to charge this purchase to my credit card.

Please check the appropriate box:
❏ Building home for myself
❏ Building home for someone else

Order Online

houseplansandmore.com

Order Toll-Free By Phone

1-800-373-2646
Fax: 314-770-2226

Express Delivery

Most orders are processed within 24 hours of receipt. If you need to place a rush order, please call us by 11:00 am CST and ask for express service.

Business Hours: Monday - Friday (7:30 am - 4:30 pm CST)

Mail Your Order

Design America, Inc.
734 West Port Plaza, Suite #208
St. Louis, MO 63146

Waterfront Home Plans

SOURCE CODE F12